CW01590417

RENEWAL

a journal of social democracy

Volume 26

1

Renewal welcomes contributions

We will consider articles from anyone involved with the process of politics and ideas. These can be in the form of new articles and essays, or 'feedback' pieces on existing published articles. We also welcome suggestions for articles and potential authors. To submit or discuss articles please email editorial@renewal.org.uk

Published by Renewal Limited
www.renewal.org.uk
in association with
Lawrence & Wishart
Central Books Building,
Freshwater Rd, Chadwell Heath, RM8 1RX

Follow Renewal on Twitter: @RENEWALjournal
Like Renewal on Facebook: https://www.facebook.com/Renewal.journal.of.social.democracy

ISSN 0968-252X
ISBN 978-1-912064-96-0

Designed by Fran Davies
Typeset by e-type, Liverpool
Printed in Devon by ImprintDigital

CONTENTS

Editorial statement

Renewal is a quarterly journal of politics and ideas, committed to exploring and expanding the emancipatory potential of social democracy.

Social democracy has always been a complex and contested political tradition. *Renewal* offers a space in which its historic purposes – the expansion of equality, democratic governance, and social freedoms – can be debated, advanced and applied to contemporary politics.

After a decade of economic stagnation and geopolitical crises, the left faces severe challenges, but also opportunities. Many on the left felt that the economic crisis of 2008 would inevitably highlight just how broken many aspects of contemporary capitalism were. But instead of riding on a tide of popular disillusionment with a failing economic model, social democracy has experienced electoral failure and cultural detachment.

This failure is neither inevitable nor irreversible. There is a developing elite consensus about the dangers posed by runaway inequality and by climate change. More importantly, there is a rising popular and cultural awareness of economic, racial and gender injustice. The right has no response to these developments, yet the left has failed to channel them into a durable political project.

The Editorial Board of *Renewal* will use the journal to create the conditions for such a project. This will mean honest, open-ended and civil confrontation across a fragmented British left. It will require an injection of new insights and ideas, drawn from international comparisons and collaboration with neglected corners of academia and activism. Finally, it demands searching critique and understanding of the political, social, economic, cultural and international contexts that will constrain and condition a new politics for the British left.

Renewal will continue to offer a focus and a gathering point for the ideas and analysis necessary to the formulation of a viable, yet radical political strategy for the twenty-first century. We invite support, and encourage contributions, from all who share that objective.

EDITORIAL

Work, autonomy, and community

Florence Sutcliffe-Braithwaite and James Stafford

Since we took on the co-editorship Renewal at the start of 2016, we have deliberately focused our efforts on filling in the conceptual gaps between academic analysis and specific policy proposals. The contributions we have sought – on Europe, inequality, community wealth, localism, democratisation and the social composition of the electorate – have been aimed at both raising the ambitions of Labour's politics and ensuring their relevance to an age of multiple crises. With the left in a strengthened position and the Labour party enjoying something of an internal truce, this issue takes the opportunity to investigate the normative foundations for a twenty-first century social democracy. Beyond the reversal of the damage caused by state austerity and corporate excess, beyond even the construction of new institutions to guarantee economic justice and ecological stability, what kinds of emancipation, what forms of life, should the left promote? Our contributors, in various ways, explore the ultimate purposes of social democracy, alongside the tensions and choices that confront us on the way. Together, they raise fundamental questions about the meaning of 'work', the value of place and community, and the realisation of social justice in the fabric of everyday life.

Communists and 'worker-ists'

Debating ideals across the famously 'broad church' of Labour and the left inevitably exposes potential divisions. One of the most fundamental of these is over the place of wage labour in a radically changed society. The conflict between the desire to improve and humanise work and to eliminate it entirely is one of the oldest fault-lines within the left, dividing socialists and social democrats along multiple axes. The coincidence of the automation revolution with the long tail of the global financial crisis has produced a situation where the nature and limits of work and wages seem like far less abstract questions than they did a decade ago. Summarising the findings of the independent Future of Work Commission he convened last year, Tom Watson MP signals scepticism of popular narratives suggesting that automation and artificial intelligence will render work as we have known it superfluous. Indeed, he defends a traditional labourist conception of work as a uniquely constructive and empowering human activity:

> Work isn't something people do to fill their time in between leisure activities, family life, and sleep, or just to pay the bills. Good work is part of our identities. It enriches our lives and enables us to be fuller and better citizens. It reminds us that we – as individuals, communities, and a society – build our own future.

Both Jo Littler and Dan Chandler, however, argue that more fundamental changes are required to ensure that the reality of wage labour can match Watson's aspirations. For Chandler, an agenda focused solely on regulation and skills is unlikely to address the fragmentation, outsourcing, and undermining of legal minimums that define the 'fissured workplaces' of the twenty-first century. Because the bargaining power of labour, as a whole, is so central, 'good work' becomes a question of macroeconomic policy.

For Littler, meanwhile, the transformation of working life will only be possible if it is embedded in an attack on the ideology of 'neoliberal meritocracy'. Frequently drawing on the language of 'diversity', this claims to tackle inequalities based on gender, race, and even (sometimes) class. But it also encourages people to marketise more and more parts of their lives, legitimising ever-rising inequalities of wealth and power. The answer lies not only in supporting and valuing all forms of work, but in developing policies and institutions that consciously work against market individualism, fostering an ethic of 'working, playing and living together, rather than competing alone'.

Thinking about work always requires us to think about gender. As part of her broader critique of a left politics that subsumes the distinctive interests of women within a homogenised 'working class', Charlotte Proudman urges Labour feminists to question the party leadership's apparent support for decriminalising the purchase of sex. Under conditions of extreme and gendered inequality, some forms of 'work' are simply not amenable to being 'monetised', still less 'civilised', on acceptable terms: the task of politics, she suggests, is to find effective means of placing them out of bounds.

The radical political economist Nick Srnicek, interviewed by Lise Butler in this issue, emphasises the possibility that automation and artificial intelligence create an opportunity to achieve a high level of freedom from the imperatives of market society. His thinking extends beyond mere techno-optimism, reaching back to nineteenth and twentieth century socialist and communist traditions, and encompassing unwaged and reproductive labour as well as the traditional wage relation. The reduction of all forms of labour can ultimately be achieved through a similar ethic of cooperation to that identified by Littler: 'experiments in collective living, social housing, the collective raising of children'.

Such an all-encompassing vision of collective freedom remains, as Srnicek concedes, a minority position within what remains a *labour* movement, where Watson's 'workerist' attitude will inevitably predominate. Yet consensus over immediate reforms – although not, perhaps, over the fraught question of the Universal Basic Income, addressed again by Malcolm Torry in this issue – remains possible. The broad front of social democrats, socialists and reformist communists assembled under the Corbyn banner can find common ground on the need to manage and contest, rather than simply resist, technological change, and to create new spaces of autonomy and dignity in a fractured and degraded labour market. No-one within the Labour party can be happy with a country where unproductive, monotonous, poorly paid employment eats up ever-more of our fellow citizens' time and energy.

Locality and the common good

Limiting the incursion of market logics into everyday life is also a focus for our articles on community, locality, and the economy. Reporting on the first phase of the New Economics Foundation's major project on the narratives we might employ to contest dominant understandings of 'the economy', Christine Berry finds broad resonance for the idea of 'common ground':

> ...the common ground story is essentially a story about priorities. It argues that the economy isn't meeting our real needs – *anyone's* real needs; that we need to look not only at how money is distributed but also at what we want that money *for*. We think this story taps into a deep sense that our society has the wrong priorities: that things like community, safety and time to enjoy life are more important than chasing growth and profits.

Like the other narrative mentioned by Berry – the 'populist story' of challenging extractive elites – a regard for the value of non-economic goods can be usefully linked to new strategies for municipal socialism and the promotion of 'community wealth'. These have been extensively outlined in *Renewal* over the past few years. Contributions from Alistair Reid, John Tomaney, and Rachel Reeves MP in this issue explore the history of 'progressive localism' as one of a number of 'alternatives to state socialism' developed within the British labour movement of the nineteenth and twentieth century. They suggest that the current consensus within Labour on the need for a decentralised political and economic system can claim a heritage within all parts of the party's diverse tradition.

Reid, in particular, draws attention to the unfairly maligned liberal strand within Labour politics. Critiquing Blue Labour's 'traditionalism' and the idea of a declining, 'left behind' working class, he argues that 'radical localism' shouldn't be reduced to 'tapping into rather fixed, traditional cultural worlds to mobilise them in support of a new national project.' Reeves, meanwhile, offers a sketch of how a radical Labour localism would break down policy silos and reach across diverse areas of the 'everyday economy', from retail and care work to credit unions, energy coops, and neighbourhood networks for the lonely and elderly.

The new spirit of socialism

What all of these writers – regardless of their factional pasts or affiliations – share is an impatience with the vision of society and selfhood implied by the dominant culture of what Littler calls 'competitive individualism'. In comparison to the party of the 1990s and 2000s, all parts of Labour today are distinctly uneasy with the idea that consumerism, competition and hyper-mobility are inescapable features of modern life. Nearly everyone also disavows Whitehall and technocracy, emphasising instead the role of local councils, community organisation, and a range of alternatives to 'state socialism'. Before the Conservatives' descent into their present confusion, Nick Timothy's intellectual influence on Theresa May kept a rival version of this story alive on the right. A gently satirical observation made in a 2014 paper by Jeremy Gilbert and the late Mark Fisher still holds true: 'today ... no mainstream politician can claim to be in favour of state action and nobody can be an avowed individualist'.[1]

It is both an irony and a promise of the current moment that so much of the programme of Labour's radical left leadership dovetails with the ambient 'neo-communitarianism' of mainstream policy elites.[2] The overall direction of this new social-democratic politics should be more radical, and more forward looking, than anything envisaged by the intellectual entrepreneurs of the early 2010s. Yet it will still be able to draw on a growing public rejection of increasingly pathological systems of neoliberal government. Whether or not all this well-intentioned localism and humanity – easy to talk about in opposition, but often difficult to sustain in government – will be able to survive contact with the complex and crisis-ridden world of the 2020s remains, of course, an open question.

Florence Sutcliffe-Braithwaite is Lecturer in Twentieth Century History at University College, London.

James Stafford is Postdoctoral Research Associate in World Politics at Bielefeld University.

Endnotes

1 M. Fisher & J. Gilbert (2014), *Reclaim Modernity: Beyond Markets, Beyond Machines*, (London, Compass).

2 W. Davies (2012), 'The Emerging Neo-Communitarianism', *The Political Quarterly*, Vol. 83, No. 4, pp767-776.

THE FUTURE OF WORK

Improving the quality of work

Tom Watson MP

The automation revolution demands an active state: one that promotes investment in new technologies while securing good jobs for all workers.

> I saw the hideous phantasm of a man stretched out, and then, on the working of some powerful engine, show signs of life and stir with an uneasy, half–vital motion.

When Mary Shelley wrote the preface to *Frankenstein* in 1831, the industrial revolution was at its height and society was being transformed by scientific developments that were taking place at a dizzying pace. In Victor Frankenstein, Shelley created a character whose enthusiasm for technological advancement and messianic determination to push the boundaries of the possible embodied the spirit of the age. But the 'uneasy, half-vital' being that Victor's experiment creates turns out to be a monster.

Frankenstein is the most famous literary expression of the unease Shelley and her contemporaries felt about the threat scientific advances posed for traditional human society.

Today, a fear similar to the one articulated so powerfully by Shelley is rooted in the belief that 'half-vital' robots will invade the workforce, take our jobs and render us redundant in a more fundamental way than simply making many of us unemployed. What societal function will we fulfil when work is carried out by someone – or something – else? How can we prepare for the changes that technological revolution will bring? Can we harness this change in order to build a fairer and more equitable society in which good work pays and bad work – including work which is less well paid, routine or mundane – is taken care of by algorithms and artificial intelligence.

For the Luddites of the early nineteenth century, this was not a philosophical question but a practical one, and they responded in uncompromising fashion by smashing up the machines they believed threatened their livelihoods. This tactic didn't work then, and it won't work now. But will the relentless march of the robots render us powerless? Or can an active state manage the transition from the industrial to the technological age and allow us to shape our own future?

I set up the Future of Work Commission, comprised of experts from academia, industry and politics, to try and answer some of these questions. It found that, although the new technological revolution is already bringing about rapid change, it could create as many jobs as it destroys. Artificial Intelligence can enhance jobs, not just gut them. Investment in the right areas can provide good jobs that are less vulnerable to automation and draw on essential human qualities that are also the hardest for machines to imitate: creativity, care, teamwork and imagination. It could even help us solve some of the economic problems that feel so intractable after eight years of Tory government: falling wages, low productivity, weak growth, inequality. These problems are the result, in large part, of poor decisions taken by Government and an ideological unwillingness to use the power of the state to address the economic challenges we face as a country.

The Commission's report concluded that the way out of this economic quagmire is to welcome automation and AI and use the levers of the state to shape the new world of work to come. Too much of the debate about technology has become dominated by a discussion about how many jobs will be lost when an army of robot labourers who don't demand holidays or claim sick pay displace their human counterparts. The question of what we want from the new world of work has received far less attention.

The Future of Work Commission was brave enough to conclude that our lives should be centred around good work. That may sound ambitious. But it is no more ambitious than the task set by the founders of the Labour party, who recognised the imbalance between workers and the people that profited from their labour and sought to address it by achieving political representation for workers. Work isn't something people do to fill their time in between leisure activities, family life and sleep or just to pay the bills. Good work is part of our identities. It enriches our lives and enables us to be fuller and better citizens. It reminds us that we – as individuals, communities, and a society – build our own future.

The centrality of work to the lives of individuals has meant it has always been central to Government and public policy makers. Administrations are judged on unemployment figures and wage increases or stagnation. The post-war consensus around full employment defined the political landscape of the time. No senior politician could hope to survive in office if unemployment figures were rising. That fact was reflected by one of the most famous political posters in UK history, Saatchi & Saatchi's Tory attack depicting a long line outside a dole office, which proclaimed 'Labour isn't working'. When Margaret Thatcher's government effectively abandoned the aim of full employment to focus instead on controlling inflation and the money supply, rocketing unemployment, and its long–term consequences in the communities worst hit by it, became one of the defining legacies of her time in office.

Employment levels and wages are critical aspects of work, but they aren't a good enough measure of the state of work in society alone. They miss a fundamental part – the quality of work.

So, the Future of Work Commission issued a rallying cry for a refocus on good work. Not just work that, as Dolly Parton says is 'all takin' and no givin'... no way to make a livin', but good work: work that is valuable in itself, that provides dignity, security and autonomy. Good work, moreover, should be available to everyone, not just the preserve of the elite while others are left with work that is poorly paid, repetitive and lacking in autonomy.

With old jobs fading away and new jobs being created all the time, focusing on creating an economy full of good work is vital. Government and public policy makers must focus on what this new world of work will look like, and on creating work that is more interesting, secure and autonomous than before. We must not just abdicate responsibility and sit back and watch what happens.

One of the Commission's key recommendations is a new Charter for Good Work, embedded in all Whitehall departments, to ensure that the creation of good work is a central objective of the Government's social and economic policy. It's not enough to continue as we have been, playing catch-up and responding to poor practice and bogus self-employment one legal challenge at a time. If the creation of good work, rather than precarious and low-paid work, is a key aim of this technological revolution, then it has to be at the heart of policymaking.

We should be measuring the quality of work too. Rather than just collecting information on unemployment, wages, productivity and GDP, we should use the OECD job quality index, which measures earnings, job security and the work environment.[1]

Any purported trade-off between 'good work' and full employment is a chimera. The OECD's view is that pursuing the objective of quality work is entirely consistent with increased productivity and high levels of employment. It will, in fact, feed both innovation and productivity.

What are the levers of the state that we can use to shape the new technological revolution and produce a future of good work?

For a start, investment. The pace of adoption of new technologies is slower in the UK than other countries and the pace is slowing. It's not just a lack of state investment, it's a failure to invest in the private sector too.

The Centre for Economic and Business Research recently found that new industrial robots installed in the UK in 2015 were down 21 per cent from 2014 levels, and that we have just 33 robots per 10,000 employees – one of the lowest ratios in OECD countries – compared to a global average of 69 per 10,000 employees.[2] An RSA report found that only 14 per cent of employers are investing in new technology or plan to do so soon, even though 43 per cent agreed that new technologies would lead to great prosperity in the long run.[3]

Investment by the UK government falls well below international competitors too. To make real progress on investment the Government needs to commit to spending the OECD average of 3.5 per cent of GDP on R&D and innovation to help support world class research and support the better use of technology by our long tail of low productivity firms. And within that increased spend, we should dedicate a percentage of the GDP to technology. We also need to make sure that innovation is more collaborative, ensuring that academia, industry and national and local government are joined up.

As Marianna Mazzucato explains in her book *The Entrepreneurial State,* the iPhone is smart because it relies on features such as Internet, GPS and touch-screen display, which were the result of long-term public investment. What she explains is that innovation is often the result of public-private partnership. Without the state-sponsored developments that Apple was able to utilise as core features of its mobile devices, consumers could have had to wait a lot longer for the 715 million iPhones currently in use around the world.

As well as more investment we need better incentives for R&D in the private sector too. Progress does require investment and, crucially, incentives and will. Companies like Apple, Intel, Deepmind and Amazon (who have plans for drone operated warehouses in the sky) have shown that there certainly is will in parts of the private sector, driven partially by profits and partially by intellectual curiosity. But motivation matters. Elon Musk might say that a desire for a greener world drives his investment in electric cars, but most entrepreneurs would say that their clear motive is profit. We need to make sure that we incentivise development in areas that will produce useful technology and good jobs.

Alongside investment, we need skills: skills to develop tech, and skills to utilise it. We also need skills that are going to be resistant to the automation revolution. The need for training extends from primary school right up to advanced research in our universities and to reskilling in the workplace.

Too many companies are not doing enough to help their employees expand and maintain their skills. Research for the Commission found that although employees were aware automation could change their jobs, they thought that changes could be positive, if only they were given the right training to adapt to that change. A survey by the trade union Usdaw found that 49 per cent of respondents felt that they had not had adequate training in the workplace. A YouGov survey, similarly, found that 55 per cent of respondents were not confident that they would be properly supported by the Government in learning new skills to adapt to changes in their role.[4]

If we are to avoid the political consequences of worker disempowerment and the decline of skilled jobs – already seen in parts of Europe and the United States – this must change. Education should be lifelong, so that when the world and work changes, all citizens are enabled to change with it.

School education needs to change too. Despite much talk from the Government about making our children's education fit for the future, school curriculums remain better suited to the analogue rather than digital age. As of last year just 11.1 per cent of students were taking Computer Science GCSE and just 12.9 per cent taking ICT. At A Level the figure is even worse. Just 1 per cent of all A Level entries are in Computing, and just 0.7 per cent are in ICT.[5]

The Government has made much of investing in AI and tech, including setting up a supposedly independent review of our AI strategy. But in evidence to a House of Lords committee in December 2017, the author of the review, Jerome Pesenti, explained that he was urged to stay away from recommendations about school-age education, being told 'looking at the curriculum is very thorny.'[6]

Just as worrying is the failure to allow students to study creative subjects alongside STEM ones. Some have pitted creative subjects against science subjects in the race for the future, but they are wrong. If our workers of the future are to be able to adapt and thrive in the rapidly changing workforce, creativity will be key.

Stian Westlake, head of policy at innovation charity Nesta, has made the point that 'It's good to invest in creative education because these are some of the skills that should be left' after the automation revolution.[7] It's important to understand what sectors and skills will be still be needed when robots are better able to do many jobs of the past. The enormous growth of the creative industries over the last few years give some indication of its strength: it is now worth £92 billion and creating jobs at four times the rate of the rest of the economy.[8] Far from being useless, creative education in schools will equip children to access these durable careers.

Other industries that require the most 'human' skills such as care should also be our focus. Despite the social care crisis caused by our ageing population, care work remains undervalued. With a critical need for more capacity in the care sector, and with little possibility of robots being able to take on significant parts of care work, we should revalue and support this sector as a major growth area. We should be taking advantage of the opportunities these automation resistant sectors offer, but at the moment we are not.

The stark reality is that Britain is woefully underprepared for the technological revolution to come. Becoming ready demands strategic planning: the policy choices we make now will shape how technological change continues to affect the work and lives of our citizens.

There isn't enough evidence that this planning is happening, or even beginning to happen. Our chronic inability as a country to spend enough on research and development is still holding us back. That is a problem today, but it will be a disaster tomorrow. We need to incentivise the adoption of new technology that will make businesses more profitable and productive. We need to focus on growth sectors that will provide good work, not work that is dehumanizing and just about pays the bills. We need to plan for and invest in the skills for a workforce that will be adaptable and innovative for years to come.

The technological revolution doesn't need to mean mass technological unemployment, but left to its own devices it might. 'Uneasy, half–vital motion' is not good enough. If we are going to seize the opportunities of this revolution, we need a Labour government to take the initiative – and soon.

This article is based on research undertaken by the Future of Work Commission, chaired by Tom Watson MP and Helen Mountfield QC. For more details of the Commission's research and membership, see www.futureofworkcommission.com.

Tom Watson is the Member of Parliament for West Bromwich East, Shadow Secretary of State for Digital, Culture, Media and Sport, and Deputy Leader of the Labour Party.

Notes

1. The OECD job quality framework relies on a wide number of databases: OECD Earnings Distribution Database for Earnings Quality; OECD Unemployment Duration database, OECD Benefit Recipients database, OECD Labour Market Programmes database and OECD Taxes and Benefits database for labour market insecurity; European Working Conditions Surveys (EWCSs) and International Social Survey Programme (ISSP) for quality of the Working Environment. See http://www.oecd.org/statistics/job-quality.htm.
2. Centre for Economics and Business Research (2017), *The impact of automation*: https://www.cebr.com/wp/wp-content/uploads/2017/03/Impact_of_automation_report_23_01_2017_FINAL.pdf.
3. B. Dellot and F. Wallace-Stephens (2017), *The Age of Automation: Artificial intelligence, robotics and the future of low-skilled work* (London: Royal Society of Arts), https://www.thersa.org/globalassets/pdfs/reports/rsa_the-age-of-automation-report.pdf.
4. Future of Work Commission (2017), *Report of the Future of Work Commission*, online at https://d3n8a8pro7vhmx.cloudfront.net/campaigncountdown/pages/1052/attachments/original/1512946196/Future_of_Work_Commission_Report__December_2017.pdf?1512946196, p.68.
5. Department of Education (2017) 'A Level and other 16 to 18 results: 2016 to 2017 (provisional)', https://www.gov.uk/government/statistics/a-level-and-other-16-to-18-results-2016-to-2017-provisional.
6. Oscar Williams, 'Government "urged" experts to water down "independent" AI review', *New Statesman*, 3 January 2018, http://tech.newstatesman.com/news/ai-review-jerome-pesenti.
7. Sarah O'Connor, 'How to robot-proof your children's careers', *Financial Times*, 6 April 2016, https://www.ft.com/content/0c7906d6-be89-11e5-9fdb-87b8d15baec2.
8. UK Creative Industries, 'Creative Industries Earn UK Almost £92 billion', November 2017, http://www.thecreativeindustries.co.uk/uk-creative-overview/news-and-views/news-creative-industries-earn-uk-almost-%C2%A392bn.

INTERVIEW: Technology, capitalism, and the future of the left

Nick Srnicek in conversation with Lise Butler

Nick Srnicek, a radical political economist based in London, has emerged as one of the major contemporary left theorists of technology and capitalism in the twenty-first century. A leading advocate of a Universal Basic Income (UBI), *his two books,* Inventing the Future (2015) *(with Alex Williams) and* Platform Capitalism (2017) *have been broadly influential, including for the current Labour leadership. His perspective is at once optimistic and cautious: recognising the potential of automation to enable a 'world without work', while warning that the left has barely begun to challenge corporate power over new technologies.*

Your work with Alex Williams, *Inventing the Future,* came out in 2015. What effect do you think it has had on the political landscape?

The book was timed well, in that it caught a wave of interest in this stuff, particularly basic income. Basic income was already being thought about by a number of different governments and being discussed by a number of different people. But what was missing was a proper left or Marxist take - there were liberal takes on the idea that emphasised work, there were right-wing takes which emphasised basic income as a replacement for the welfare state, but there wasn't a Marxist take saying here's why basic income can be quite a powerful tool for the working class. So, I think our book is unique in that way, tying together ideas about 'surplus population', ideas about technological change in capitalism, and a response that could nicely solve some of these issues.

The other thing I think we contributed to was not just basic income, but the broader post-work idea - things like the reduced working week, for example, which is now gaining a lot more interest. Some major unions in Germany are now pushing for a 28-hour work week, and there's a number of think tanks here in the UK that have started to think about the impact of a shorter working week on wages and productivity.

The last thing I think the book has contributed to, is maybe the arguments around organisation. The book helped some people to articulate what had gone wrong with the left in terms of the way it has organised from the late nineties to up to 2010 or so, and why it was unable to generate any significant change. I like to think the book has had some impact in pushing people towards the hybrids – between party and movements – that are being developed now. Momentum is a good example of this, with its explicit commitment to the Labour Party, but also with its interest in carrying out activities that we'd typically associate with social movements or more activist groups. I think the future of effective political organisation is something much messier than just the horizontal/vertical binary that's dominated left thinking for some time now.

Discussions about the current state and future of work have become increasingly mainstream over the last few years. On the left, there are multiple initiatives grappling with automation and the gig economy, such as Tom Watson's Future of Work Commission, and projects by the IPPR and the Fabian Society. Do you think that these initiatives have correctly diagnosed the problems we're facing, and have begun to propose workable solutions? If not, why not?

I think there's a necessary limitation to these recent proposals, which is that they're nationally focused, and self-consciously so. But we're now trying to solve a global problem, and a global issue of surplus populations and automation which affects not just the developed world but also developing countries. Actually, automation will more significantly affect developing countries, because a lot of the jobs that have been outsourced to these countries are jobs that are quite easy to automate: low-wage manufacturing, low-wage service jobs, repetitive jobs that don't require a lot of creativity. Most estimates say that the impact of automation is going to be much worse in a country like Nigeria than it is in the UK.

This challenges a traditional pathway of development for these countries - the idea that you go from an agricultural based society to an industrialised manufacturing based economy, eventually moving to a de-industrialised service-based economy. What happens when you can't industrialise because the robots are doing all those jobs? That's a really big question for a lot of developing countries, and a really big question for development economics that not a lot of people are thinking about right now (with some exceptions like Dani Rodrik, who has been talking about premature de-industrialisation). I think that problem has not been grappled with at all by think tanks in rich countries, who are worried about their own citizens.

Do you have any interest in the proposals and ideas emerging from the Future of Work Commission?

Anything that's based upon the centrality of work and getting more people into jobs is not an adequate answer. I think the changing nature of capitalism means that it is increasingly unable to generate sufficient good jobs. The UK economy, for instance, can produce a lot of jobs but most of them are terrible. We've got lots of self-employment, lots of precarious work, lots of low-wage jobs, lots of in-work poverty. We don't have a lot of good jobs. And if we get any automation or any productivity increases in the British economy, then you'd have all these people unemployed because robots would be taking their jobs.

So, I think that's the choice today. Either you have higher unemployment and a higher productivity economy, or you have a low productivity, low wage, high employment economy like the UK has. Neither of them are particularly desirable. Neither are solved by trying to get people more jobs, because global capitalism is heading into a low-growth trajectory. We need to be thinking instead about how we can eliminate our reliance upon jobs.

How will Brexit interact with automation? Are we going to see a re-nationalisation of industrial production enabled by new technology?

There are two different tendencies at play here. One is that Brexit leads to less immigration, which leads to fewer workers, and therefore leads to a demand for more automation. You have an insufficient supply of workers, so you need robots to do your jobs. The other tendency, though, which is opposed to that, is uncertainty about the economy: the lack of growth in the economy and the lack of profits for companies means they just don't want to invest in anything. So, they don't end up putting any money into automation, and they end up firing workers as the economy falls behind and possibly heads into recession. I think that second tendency is likely to be more dominant. Which means that the end result is, again, a low productivity, low wage, increasingly low-employment economy, as people suddenly get laid off. I think that's the most likely medium-term outcome of Brexit.

What do you think of proposals made for example by the IPPR for using worker ownership and sovereign wealth funds to create universal basic income based on capital dividends from firms rather than redistribution through the state? Is this a superior alternative, is it merely complimentary, or is it the wrong approach?

One thing that Alex and I never talked about when writing *Inventing the Future,* and we haven't talked about enough since, is the ownership issue, which I think is absolutely crucial.

What really frightened the capitalists in the 1970s was workers with a lot of strength suddenly pushing for ownership and control. The Meidner plan in Sweden, the Institute for Workers' Control and National Enterprise Board in the UK, *Strukturpolitik* in Germany: all of these were attempts to give workers ownership and democratic control over significant chunks of the economy. These ideas were part of a key strategic moment that actually could have gone beyond social democracy as we know it. There could have been a much greater change in capitalism, which contained the potential to move beyond it altogether. Capitalists recognised this at the time, and put their full force behind rejecting any application of these ideas. All of this illustrates how important ownership and democratic control are, and these sorts of proposals need to be updated and extended for our current times. IPPR is, I think, doing absolutely essential work on that sort of stuff.

To what extent do you think that the Corbyn leadership is grappling with the changing nature of work and the implications of automation?

I think that they fully get it, actually. I think the people around Corbyn understand this stuff, are paying attention to it, and are interested in radical solutions. You see this, for instance, with the 'New Economics' event series put on by McDonnell. They are continually inviting in people to offer radical ideas, and then they are going out and trying to broaden the public discourse around these ideas as well. Which is what makes me optimistic about them, actually. I think they are aware of the current conjuncture. I think they are aware that traditional solutions won't work.

I also think they're aware of the challenges that will happen once they get into power. The war-gaming by McDonnell to prepare for potential capital flight is exactly what you want to do if you're preparing to try some radical ideas. A friend of mine has raised an important limit though, which is that Labour may recognise the threat from capital, but do they recognise the threat from conservative trade unions?

That's one area that may be overlooked at the present moment: what happens when trade unions are the ones who are holding back progress? Which I think is very likely to happen. We see it already with the dominant trade union reaction to immigration, which is to close up into a national bubble that blames foreigners for low wages. It's a complete abdication of basic leftist principles of international solidarity, and it harms every worker by playing them off against each other. I worry that a Corbyn government hasn't planned for the reactionary tendencies of some trade unions, and that they wouldn't be willing to take on those sorts of conservative stances.

Have you noticed more progressive moves on the part of trade unions? I know that the Fabian Society have set up the Changing Work Centre in partnership with the Community union. There's trade union presence on the Future of Work Commission. Could you take a more optimistic view of the role of trade unions in debates about the changing nature of work?

At the leadership level, I don't have any optimism. I think it's very much stuck in an old mindset: work is the ultimate good and that's the only thing they're able to provide. For them, the fight against automation is a fight to save jobs rather than a fight for free time. That being said, whenever I give a talk and I have union members come up to me afterwards, younger ones seem very interested in these sorts of ideas. I think that there is a generational difference there as well, that the older generation is stuck in very traditional workerist ideals, while the younger generation realises what's going on, realises that these old solutions aren't going to work, and they're quite interested in alternative ways out. So, I'm hopeful maybe in the medium term, but in the short term, no.

Fears about the impact of automation and optimistic visions for a post-work society, including ideas for universal basic income, have a long history. Do have any thoughts on why these debates disappeared from the political mainstream after the 1960s and 1970s? Do you think today's debates about work and automation will have more staying power?

I think there are economic reasons and cultural reasons that these debates didn't end up going anywhere. These debates around robots taking all of our jobs re-occur every twenty years or so. People mock that repetition and say, well, what's to worry about, because we've had these fears before and they didn't turn out. I think that's the wrong way to look at it, because what happens is that the jobs that people are worried about *do* disappear. Manufacturing jobs *did* disappear, for instance. What was missed was that manufacturing jobs were replaced with service jobs – and there was a massive transformation in work and our relation to it. Just focusing on aggregate job numbers over long-term periods misses that. So you get this cyclical moment where a section of jobs are automated (or outsourced) and ideas about how to solve that problem become widely discussed. But then new jobs appear in some other sector, and despite the pain that transformation may cause for many people, the new jobs settle the question of what is to be done: get people into jobs, as we've always done.

The other reason for that earlier shift from post-work ideas is the cultural barriers they ran into, and I think this is particularly the case in the United States. In the 1960s and 1970s, they were talking about a basic income, it was quite popular, and Nixon was thinking about implementing one, but they didn't end up going with it because of the ways it was framed. The problem was that the salient categories that grounded welfare – the deserving/undeserving poor, most notably – were ignored by the basic income proposal. Everyone was equivalent in the policy's view, and everyone was deserving. But some groups of people – particularly white 'deserving' poor – resented being conflated with others – particularly black 'undeserving' poor. The racial divisions here meant that even though they would have benefited from the proposal, the white poor tended to reject the policy because they saw it as stigmatising them. The end result is that the policy lost traction, some of the more pressing social crises abated, and the more radical solutions fell to the side.

The changing structure of capitalism also made some of those earlier worries about automation seem irrelevant. There was massive chaos throughout the 1970s, and then a relatively stable replacement by neoliberalism from the 1980s onwards. This provided people with enough jobs, with low wages but sufficient amounts of money (plus lots of extra credit) to be able to produce higher living standards. I think that was the solution to that crisis at that point in time. But there are bigger secular tendencies to capitalism that were obscured by the relative cyclical rebound after the 1970s. The trendline for growth amongst all the advanced capitalist countries has been in decline since then, and we've seen another dip in trendline growth since the 2008 crisis. And without growth, it becomes near impossible to try and return to the social democratic consensus which was, crucially, a consensus between labour and capital in the context of a unique period of rapid economic growth.

One of the major tendencies that we should/could have noticed earlier is the creation of 'surplus populations'. There's an interesting intellectual history to tell here too. The Marxist concepts of immiseration and the industrial reserve army – which suggested that capitalism would lead to workers facing worse conditions and outright expulsion from the economic cycle – were quite prominent prior to social democracy, the Second World War, and the welfare state. But then in the 1950s, 1960s and 1970s they completely disappeared from most Marxist research because you have high-wage jobs, people working a lot, and it seems like capitalism can produce a sustainable consensus.

Notably though, the idea of 'surplus populations' stays with those who are facing the sharp end of capitalism - particularly with black Marxists, postcolonial thinkers, and feminist thinkers. They're the ones arguing that surplus populations and immiseration are essential parts of the crisis tendencies of capitalism. But for rich countries, for white, middle class men, it doesn't seem to be a major issue anymore, and so those traditional notions of capitalism's crisis tendencies tend to fade away.

In the last decade or so, I think we've seen a return of these earlier ideas as a way to make sense of contemporary conditions. I think Fredric Jameson sums this up well when he declares *Capital* to be a book about unemployment – an idea that would have seemed absurd fifteen years ago, but seems like an incisive point now. The idea of a settled consensus for capitalism is completely gone, and it's increasingly obvious that capitalism produces a significant surplus population. I guess what I'm trying to say is that much of today's situation was eminently foreseeable, if only you were looking at the right thinkers!

Moving on to your more recent *Platform Capitalism*, what was the intellectual journey that led you to from *Inventing the Future* to this book?

Platform Capitalism was originally going to be almost a direct extension of *Inventing the Future*. It was going look at how different technologies – not just automation technologies but things like the Internet of Things, 3D printing, all these new technologies – how they could be deployed in a post-capitalist world, what they would mean. But when I started to look at it more and more, I realised that there wasn't a critical take that engaged with this stuff from a political economy perspective. There was plenty of cultural critique and political critique, but no systematic take on how these related to changing conditions of capitalism. I also kept seeing the idea of platforms re-appearing over and over again, but I was never clear on what people were talking about. It seemed to have a different meaning for every author. In many ways the book was written as a way to clarify what that term means, and how it fits into a broader context of capitalism?

The other thing I wanted to analyse was the tendency for people to announce a massive new shift in capitalism. Contemporary academic production seems to demand that everyone declare radical shifts in order to brand an idea, but I wanted to take a more sensible, sober look at whether or not that's true, and what exactly is happening with platforms.

So that's what the book was all about: to ask what are platforms? How do they fit into a broader history of capitalism and how do they change capitalism? Is it a completely new type of capitalism, or is it something which is a continuation of earlier trends?

What's the relationship between 'platforms' and artificial intelligence?

The economic impacts of artificial intelligence are today often talked about solely via its effect on automation, the idea that artificial intelligence can, to give one example, eliminate the need for human translators. But I think the more interesting effects of AI have to do with the internal structure of companies, intra-capitalist competition, and how they're reengineering the macro structure of the economy.

What's really interesting to me is in the past year or two, Google has started announcing itself in interviews as an AI-first company. It no longer positions itself as a search engine company. Likewise, Amazon is turning into an AI-first company. Facebook is turning into an AI-first company. Alibaba is turning into an AI-first company. There's a sort of convergence amongst all these major platforms, towards AI being their dominant focus.

I think this is for a couple of reasons. One is that only these major companies can do AI. The way that we do AI today, through machine learning, requires a lot of data. So, you have to throw a lot of data into these algorithms, train them, and then they can do these tasks. That means only companies with a lot of data can do it, which happens to be these major platforms that have been collecting all this data. So a handful of companies that can do AI are now competing against each other to have control over artificial intelligence, which allows them to improve their services and gain competitive advantage that way.

On current trends, I think AI will become something that will be owned by a few companies, and will be rented out to everyone else as a fee-based service. Every other company in the world will need it: it will be crucial to survive in the future of capitalism. But it will be dominated by one or two suppliers, Amazon and Google most likely (at least in the Western world). And that, I think, is a really interesting shift in intra-capitalist competition, is that these companies recognise the significance of AI as a general-purpose technology which isn't just applied to social media and search engines, but can also be applied to any industry in the world. It's going to be a crucial economic infrastructure, and a crucial tool of political power in the future. That's why I think Google sees itself as an AI-first company. That's why I think Amazon is interested in Alexa and stuff like that. They want all this data. They want to be able to train their algorithms, so they can have dominance five or ten years down the line.

Is there anything we can do about that?

One thing here is ownership over data. If you start thinking about who owns that data and it's not just immediately assumed that companies own that data, then it becomes much more difficult for them to be able to control the data, monopolise it, and build up systems of dominance.

I'll give an example: something like health data. You might train an algorithm on health data to be able to pick up, say, the likelihood of a tumour that's cancerous or not. Clearly a useful application of these technologies. If the ownership of that data is with the public, it should change the ownership status of any algorithm or app or service derived from the data. Rather than thinking about Google, for instance, as owning the data, the hardware/software to train algorithms, and the eventual user-facing products built from them – we might instead conceive of Google's role as something more akin to an algorithmic factory. Their training of an algorithm is a process which turns raw publicly-owned data into something which is more readily usable. They could easily be contracted and remunerated for performing this work on the original data, but with the proviso that the end product would have ownership maintained by the public whose data it is derived from. That's one way to push back against these companies that have control of it all. But solutions to these problems are an incredibly difficult thing to think about, and I think we're only at the beginning stages.

You conclude *Platform Capitalism* by suggesting that rather than just regulating corporate platforms, efforts should be made to create public platforms, platforms that are controlled by the people. How might said public platforms work?

The first thing to say is that I don't think there's any general approach. The idea that I have in mind is something like public ownership over these platforms. And I say *public* ownership because that doesn't necessarily mean national ownership. It could be local or cooperative ownership. It could be a regional thing, it could be an international thing. I think the scale is completely open for debate.

The other aspect is what it would mean to publicly own Facebook is different to what it would mean to publicly own Google, which is different to what it would mean to publicly own Uber. I don't think there's any general theory for public ownership of these companies. Each one of these platforms is quite significantly different. With something like Uber, it's relatively easy to imagine a publicly-owned, TFL version that serves the people and is not for profit. Maybe something like a social network that is publicly owned, we can imagine that relatively easily. But then we start thinking about a search engine, it becomes a bit more difficult, or a global AI-first company? The challenges mount as we start to move up the hierarchy of platforms and as their global nature becomes more central to how they operate.

You say – in brackets – that public platforms should be 'independent of the surveillance state'. How could this independence be established?

I think the point about the surveillance state is really important as well. How do we technologically and legally separate these data intensive platforms from a surveillance state that wants all this data? The nightmare scenario is something like China's social credits system that they're building, where all of this data that they're collecting from social media then gets filtered into the government, and then they give you a credit score on the basis of that, about how good of a citizen you are, and that determines parts of your life. (It's worth mentioning that many Western data brokers already do something like this.) That seems like a nightmare scenario, but it seems all-too plausible if the surveillance state and platforms are combined together.

We need two things at least: one is the legal rules to maintain separation, and there's a really good precedent here, which is the postal system. This is a system of public communication where people are transferring information between each other, which is often nationally owned and run. But we have legal rules in place in that the government can't just open up any piece of mail and look into it. And it's worked really well. So, we can do that in the same way with internet communications; it's the same sort of principles.

I think we also need technical rules as well. How do we build up firewalls between what the government can access and what we're doing online? There is encryption, for instance, and all these things that can make it incredibly difficult. There are ways to do it but we have to think about those and include those as well.

Does the political will exist, in your view, to make any of these changes, or to bring any of this to greater public scrutiny?

I never really liked the idea of political will, which is a bit too voluntarist for me. I think the relevant point is more about the conditions which are being shaped more and more towards this movement arising. Just in the past year, the amount of scrutiny that tech companies have faced is drastically different from two years ago. Two years ago, if you asked people what are the top, most loved brands: YouTube, Facebook, Amazon would have been up there. Now, there's a lot of discontent with those platforms. More people are becoming aware of the monopolising tendencies of these things. More people are recognising the amount of data they're collecting, and the implications of that as well. More people are learning about their political impacts, and these platforms are now starting to be challenged from all sides politically when they take a perceived wrong step. I think this is all inevitable for these companies for the very simple reason that they've becoming more woven into the everyday fabric of life. Whereas they were once a relatively bounded part of society, today they are becoming a common infrastructure, with the consequence that their actions are more heavily scrutinised.

Thanks so much for speaking with us Nick. To conclude, what are you working on now?

Helen Hester and I are finishing up a book called *After Work: The Fight for Free Time*. It is going to be out next year, and it'll be discussing social reproduction and post-work politics. The guiding idea being that post-work politics talks about waged work a lot, and it often tends to talk about male waged work a lot. It doesn't talk about unwaged work very much but this means that it misses a huge amount of work that society undertakes.

One of the things we've been finding, for instance, is that when you look at the amount of work time that is done in countries – the number of hours devoted to waged and unwaged labour – it's about 45 per cent unwaged and 55 per cent waged. So, if you just talk about post-work in terms of waged labour, you're missing almost half of the work that is being done in society, even just on a quantitative, simple measure. So, we want to talk about what it means for post-work politics to apply to social reproduction. But the challenge there is that most of that work can't easily be automated, either because technically it can't be automated or morally we don't want to automate it. So the question driving the book is how do you apply post-work ideas to that sort of work?

We've got a few broad ideas. The first one is to make finer distinctions about automation. So, when you talk about the automation of care work, people typically think, 'No, you can't automate care work'. But that's such a blunt distinction between care work and non-care work. When you actually talk to care workers who do it for a living, and ask could particular tasks of your job be automated? They will say, actually, yes, a lot of their job could be automated. If your job is to look after elderly people, for example, then you might think about automating the task of organising and distributing medication for people. That could be automated easily and it would free elder care workers to do more human based work, rather than just a mechanical sorting of medication.

We also need to think about the social organisation of this work. Today it's centred upon the nuclear family, it's centred upon individual households, and that's such an inefficient and crude way to organise this work. In the book we're returning to these early 1900s communist arguments and experiments in collective living, social housing, the collective raising of children, and so on. On the basis of that, we're arguing that if you're going to build social housing today, maybe don't do it in an individualised way, but think about it in a collective way.

So you subscribe to those sorts of ideas?

Yes. Collective kitchens, collective theatre, collective maker spaces – so everyone can have a 3D printer they can all use. We can update these traditional ideas for the twenty-first century, but the same sorts of principles can again help us reduce the amount of labour we need to do.

Our third broad idea is the management of living standards. There is this interesting tendency in the history of domestic technologies where something like the dishwasher comes in, and you'd think it's going to reduce the amount of work that gets done, but what actually happens is that the standards of cleanliness just go up and up and up. And so it doesn't actually reduce work, it just means that the standards get higher, and you have to keep dishes and clothes and the house cleaner than you ever had to beforehand. Over the course of the twentieth century, the amount of housework done per person has barely budged, despite all the new technologies introduced. This ratcheting up of standards tends to subtly intervene everywhere. Even when you look at a lot of post-work writing, oftentimes they'll talk about how glorious it will be that we can make these fantastic meals, once we don't have to worry about our jobs anymore.

We should recognise that this is a subtle re-imposition of work: that we need to make fantastic meals for all our friends, which can be great for some people who love cooking, but a nightmare for those who don't. We have to be wary about this re-imposition of higher and higher standards which compels us to do more and more social work. Childcare is a really good example as well. There's an interesting phenomenon in recent decades where parents are doing more and more waged work, but childcare hours are also going up – precisely the opposite of what you would expect. And that's because the competitive demands of contemporary childcare are forcing parents to ever more tightly manage their children's lives in some desperate attempt to optimise the perfect child. We need to be aware of these tendencies (and in this case, their market-driven origins) and we need to think about how to manage it in some sense. And that will help us reduce the work that goes into social reproduction as well. So those three things are some of the ways in which we can think about applying post-work to social reproduction.

Nick Srnicek is Lecturer in Digital Economy at Kings College London.

Lise Butler is Lecturer in Modern History at City, University of London.

Speenhamland, automation, and Basic Income: A response

Malcolm Torry

In our last issue, Frederick Pitts, Lorena Lombardozzi and Neil Warner criticised the idea of a Basic Income on the grounds that it might function as a depressive subsidy to low wages. Here a leading advocate responds with the argument that Basic Income functions differently to a simple wage subsidy.

In the final edition of *Renewal* for 2017 (issue 25.3-4), Frederick Pitts, Lorena Lombardozzi and Neil Warner suggest that the experience of the Speenhamland reforms of 1795 were 'an experiment in a kind of basic income'.[1]

It was not. It was an extension of poor relief to the working poor. The supplements paid out of the rates guaranteed a net income. They were definitely not a 'Basic Income'. The difference is crucial. A guaranteed minimum income is a minimum income level below which a household's income is not allowed to fall, and the payment made is designed to bring a household's net income up to the specified level. The modern equivalents are Working Tax Credits and so-called Universal Credit. In Speenhamland the supplement paid out was designed to fill the gap between the worker's earnings and a specified minimum income that was related to the size of the family and to the price of bread. The supplement was a means-tested benefit.

A Basic Income is entirely different. It is an equal payment to every individual of the same age. The difference is clear. The Speenhamland payments fell if earnings rose, and rose if earnings fell. A Basic Income remains the same whatever the individual's earnings. This means that the effects are very different. The Speenhamland supplement functioned as a dynamic subsidy. It rose if wages fell, so employers who cut wages knew that the supplement would make up for the wage cut. A Basic Income would be a static subsidy: that is, it would not rise if wages fell, so both employers and employees would know that if wages fell then employees' families would be worse off. Both collective bargaining and the National Living Wage would be even more important than they are now, and the effort to maintain them would intensify.

Another difference relates to employment incentive. Within the communities that were paying the Speenhamland supplement, for a large family with a single low-wage breadwinner there was no financial advantage to seeking increased wages, or to seeking a better-paying job, or to seeking additional skills. Increased wages would mean a lower supplement. But because a Basic Income would never change, anyone currently on means-tested benefits whose Basic Income enabled them to come off them would immediately experience increased incentives to seek higher wages, or to seek additional skills in order to obtain a better-paying job. No longer would an increase in wages result in a loss of benefits, so an increase in earned income would result in a far greater increase in net income.[2]

Pitts, Lombardozzi and Warner are quite right to make a variety of criticisms of the Speenhamland approach. Means-tested in-work benefits such as the Speenhamland supplements, Working Tax Credits, and Universal Credit, do 'keep the cost of labour competitive with machines so that employers keep workers hanging on for longer than otherwise would be the case';[3] they do restrict 'the freedom of workers to sell their capacity to labour to employers as equal parties to a contract'(p149); and they do 'render impossible the commodification of labour in a world still organised on the basis of the commodification of everything else'(p150). A Basic Income, on the other hand, would never compromise 'the bargaining power of labour', and so would not contribute to 'falling or stagnating wages and deteriorating employment prospects'(p151). Indeed, by providing a secure financial platform on which individuals and households could build, a Basic Income would increase workers' ability to start their own businesses, to turn down badly-paid jobs, and to argue for wage increases.

The Basic Income enthusiasts that Pitts, Lomardozzi and Warner have in their sights are those who suggest that a Basic Income would be a useful response to an automated economy in which fewer human workers would be required. It needs to be said that we cannot know the future of the employment market. Previous periods of technological change have seen new jobs created at the same time as existing jobs have been destroyed. The fact that we cannot know the future shape of the employment market that is the argument for Basic Income. The benefits system that we are running in the UK is still a combination of the Poor Law and Speenhamland – that is, means-tested benefits both in and out of work. It is a system designed for a 1940s employment market characterised by long-term full-time jobs. This is even more true of Universal Credit. But the world has changed, and it will continue to change in ways that we cannot now predict. What we shall need is an income maintenance strategy that makes no assumptions about the future structure of the employment market that incentivises employment, that provides as much freedom as possible for workers to choose how to deploy their labour, and that does not depress wages. Today's benefits system is precisely what is not required. A Basic Income might be the best option.

The debate about Basic Income is important, so it needs to be rational. Rational debate requires careful definition and attention to detail. A Basic Income is an unconditional and nonwithdrawable income paid to each individual. The Speenhamland supplements were very different. What the current debate requires is not erroneous comparisons but high-quality research and careful logic.

Dr. Malcolm Torry is Director of the Citizen's Basic Income Trust, and a Visiting Senior Fellow at the London School of Economics, and is the author of *Money for Everyone: Why we need a Citizen's Income* (Policy Press, 2013), *101 Reasons for a Citizen's Income* (Policy Press, 2015), *The Feasibility of Citizen's Income* (Palgrave Macmillan, 2016), and *Citizen's Basic Income: A Christian social policy* (Darton, Longman and Todd, 2016). A second edition of *Money for Everyone* with a new title, *Why we need a Citizen's Basic Income*, will be published by Policy Press later this year. He writes here in a personal capacity, and the views expressed are not necessarily those of the Citizen's Basic Income Trust.

Notes

1 F.H.Pitts, L.Lomardozzi, & N.Warner, 'Speenhamland, automation and the basic income: A warning from history?' *Renewal*, 25/3-4, 2017, p.150.

2 On the number of households that would be released from means-tested benefits by a feasible illustrative Basic Income scheme, and on the reduction that the scheme would secure in an important marginal deduction rate, see M.Torry, *A variety of indicators evaluated for two implementation methods for a Citizen's Basic Income*, Euromod working paper 12/17, Institute for Social and Economic Research, University of Essex, Colchester, 2017, www.iser.essex.ac.uk/research/publications/working-papers/euromod/em12-17.

3 Pitts et al, 'Speenhamland, automation and the basic income', p.149.

The disintegrated firm

Dan Chandler

Since the 1980s, vertically integrated firms have increasingly given way to more varied and fissured workplaces, contributing to the growth of poorly paid and precarious work, and to deteriorating working conditions. David Weil's book analyses what can be done.

D. Weil, *The Fissured Workplace*, Cambridge, MA, Harvard University Press, 2014

We are living through a transformation of work. Technology is changing the content of the jobs we do, as machines replace humans in some tasks while changing the nature of others, with important consequences for employment and inequality.[1] But technology is also changing the organisation of work: the way that tasks are bundled into jobs, the way that jobs and workers are organised into firms, and the nature of the employment relationship between firms and workers. Changes in the organisation of work, and their implications for inequality, have risen up the political agenda in recent years, spurred by the rise of platforms like Uber and Deliveroo, and of the 'gig economy' more broadly.[2] But these changes are best understood as the latest manifestation of a longer-term transformation which has been underway since the 1980s.

This longer-term transformation is the focus of David Weil's important book, *The Fissured Workplace*. Weil, an academic and recognised expert in employment and labour market policy, argues that for much of the twentieth century the economic landscape was dominated by large integrated firms ('lead firms'), where most of the activities and workers involved in producing a good or service were located within the boundaries of a single firm. Since the 1980s, lead firms have increasingly shed activities and direct employment through a range of new organisational models, from subcontracting, to franchising, to the development of complex domestic and international supply chains. Weil argues that these changes have delivered benefits to consumers through lower prices, and investors through higher returns. But they have come at a substantial cost to workers, contributing to the growth of poorly paid and precarious work, and to deteriorating job quality and working conditions.

Weil's book is perhaps the first to bring such a wide range of organisational forms within a single descriptive and analytical framework, and its greatest strength is the way he draws out the underlying economic logic which explains both the rise of the 'fissured workplace' and its consequences for workers. Weil highlights two key forces behind the rise of the 'fissured workplace'. First, advances in technology such as barcodes and scanners have made it cheaper to communicate with and monitor third parties. These changes have allowed firms to reap the benefits of the market while maintaining product and service quality. Second, Weil highlights increased pressure from capital markets for firms to reduce costs, driven by the growth of private equity, increasingly sophisticated institutional investors, and a widespread faith in the benefits of focusing on 'core competencies'.

Weil's principal concern is the implications of these changes for workers. Much of the book is spent documenting the ways in which supplier firms have responded to intense competitive pressure by flouting labour laws in order to reduce costs. He cites evidence of widespread violations of health, safety and minimum wage laws, and misclassification of workers to avoid social contributions, alongside case studies which bring home the disastrous consequences for workers. Weil also argues that fissuring is changing the distribution of resources in more fundamental ways. His starting point – building on a growing body of theoretical and empirical work in economics – is that firms typically generate economic rents (firms like Apple, for example, may benefit from a degree of monopoly power), and share these rents with employees for a variety of reasons. Weil argues that by moving certain groups of workers outside the boundaries of the lead firm, fissuring reduces their share of these rents.

A number of quantitative studies have confirmed that low-skilled service workers receive lower wages than their in-house counterparts.[3] However, the exact mechanism remains up for debate. For example, supplier firms typically have very little bargaining power vis-a-vis lead firms, and so have little by way of rents to share with workers. But alongside such structural reasons, Weil emphasises cultural forces, in particular the role of fairness norms. He argues that the wages a worker is willing to accept will depend on what others are being paid in the same firm. As a result, large firms with a mix of high and low skilled workers may compress wages, pulling up wages for low skilled workers. If fissuring splits high and low skilled workers into separate specialised firms, low skilled workers may lose out.

What can be done? The most obvious harm caused by fissuring is the way in which it has allowed firms to evade and undermine legal minimums, and fixing this is the centre of Weil's policy discussion. While he is focused on the US, the basic principles are relevant for the UK, and cover some similar ground to Matthew Taylor's recent review of 'modern working practices'.[4] First, we need to clarify legal responsibilities to reflect new realities. For example, lead firms could be held jointly responsible for violations by their suppliers, reflecting the degree to which they control suppliers' behaviour. We also need to remove legal loopholes and perverse incentives: in the UK this means clarifying the different categories of worker, and abolishing tax advantages for self-employment. Second, we need more robust enforcement: both more resources, and using these resources more effectively by focusing on lead firms, leveraging their incentive to protect their reputations, and their capacity to enforce standards. Finally, we cannot and should not rely on formal policing alone: we need to empower workers to exercise voice in the workplace through unions and access to employment tribunals.

Weil's policy discussion is detailed and well argued, and would help stamp out the worst abuses. But it does not address the wider relationship between fissuring and inequality which he identifies. Weil is right to argue that we cannot turn back the clock, but what can we do about the bigger structural landscape? One option is to reduce the rents enjoyed by lead firms through competition and tax policy – policies advocated by Joseph Stiglitz.[5] More broadly, we need to think about policies which can reduce inequality: raising the productivity of low skilled workers through education policy and industrial strategy, and strengthening workers' bargaining power through stronger unions and workers on boards. Finally, if the market is delivering an increasingly unequal distribution, we need to think more seriously about redistribution, whether through traditional tax and transfer policies, or more radical options such as a Universal Basic Income, which would also strengthen workers' bargaining power.

Looking forward, fissuring is likely to expand in breadth – reaching beyond low-skilled services into professions like law, journalism and finance – and in depth, as platforms and the 'gig economy' take fissuring to a whole new level. These changes are likely to further weaken the employment relationship and increase inequality. These trends raise some deep questions: what is the proper balance of responsibilities between employers, workers and the state for things like training, workplace injuries, parental benefits and wider income security? Should we respond to inequality by attempting to shape the distribution of market incomes ('predistribution') or through greater redistribution? Answering these questions, with an open mind to radical new solutions, should be an urgent priority for progressive politics.

Dan Chandler is a doctoral researcher in economics at the LSE.

Notes

1 D.Autor, 'Why Are There Still So Many Jobs? The History and Future of Workplace Automation', *Journal of Economic Perspectives*, 2015.

2 For an interesting discussion, see A.Sundararajan, *The Sharing Economy: The End of Employment and the Rise of Crowd-Based Capitalism*, Cambridge: MIT Press, 2016.

3 A.Dube, & E.Kaplan, 'Does Outsourcing Reduce Wages in the Low-Wage Service Occupations? Evidence from Janitors and Guards', *Industrial & Labor Relations Review*, 2010; D.Goldschmidt, & J.Schmieder, 'The Rise of Domestic Outsourcing and the Evolution of the German Wage Structure', Forthcoming in *Quarterly Journal of Economics*, 2018.

4 M.Taylor, 'Good Work: The Taylor Review of Modern Working Practices', 2017, https://www.gov.uk/government/uploads/system/uploads/attachment_data/file/627671/good-work-taylor-review-modern-working-practices-rg.pdf.

5 J.E.Stiglitz, *Rewriting the Rules of the American Economy: An Agenda for Growth and Shared Prosperity*, London: W. W. Norton & Company, 2015.

NARRATIVES AND VALUES

Young and old meritocracy: from radical critique to neoliberal tool

Jo Littler

Since the 1970s a neoliberal form of meritocracy has become the basic common sense of British society. But it needs challenging, for all this meritocratic system does is justify hierarchies and vast inequalities, and marketise more and more of life. A socialist alternative should value diversity and democracy, and, above all, tackle economic inequality.

In January 2018, Toby Young stepped down from the board of the new Office for Students (OFS), the government's new regulatory body for higher education in England. This occurred after a widespread public outcry at his appointment, including an online petition calling for his removal with more than 200,000 signatures. Young's support for eugenics, his continual tweeting about 'tits' (including those of female MPs and fourteen-year old girls), his disparagement of wheelchair access ramps and his condemnation of state school pupils as 'stains' was the kind of humour whose sense of infantile superiority appealed to a particular type of public schoolboy and *The Spectator*, but was offensive to most – primarily because it essentially functioned by disparaging absolutely everyone beyond it; everyone apart from wealthy white public schoolboys. There were few groups Young had *not* offended, which made it harder for the right to defend his position, (although Theresa May and Kirstie Allsopp tried).

A Tory pundit and a chum of Jo and Boris Johnson, Young has been a key activator of the privatised 'free' school agenda and, since 2017, has been Chief Operating Officer of the New Schools Network, an organisation given large amounts of money by the government to establish schools outside of local authority control. His appointment to the OFS, like the constitution of the OFS itself, has been accurately read by some commentators as not simply another attempt to extend the structures of privatisation (although of course it was), but as an ideological intervention attempting to ignite a 'culture war' within universities – to drag them towards the right by challenging the politics of speakers and lecturers at a time when young people are more left wing than they have been for generations.[1] Though the OFS and the May government continue, Young's sacking has been an energising minor victory against the Tories' misogynistic right-wing populism and Trump-lite politics.

A sizeable amount of the media coverage of the Toby Young debacle mentioned his father Michael Young, the sociologist and inventive social entrepreneur who co-founded the Open University and the Consumer's Association, and respected Labour grandee who penned the 1945 Labour Party manifesto. Media profiles on the OFS affair frequently highlighted Toby Young's desire and inability to live up to his father's flamboyant reputation, and the political differences between Youngs senior and junior.[2] In particular, many pieces foregrounded the connections and differences between Toby and Michael on one specific subject: meritocracy.

'Meritocracy' today is generally understood to involve the idea that a fair social system is one in which people can work hard, activate their talent and achieve social success. This credo has come to be 'common sense' within modern society. There is more-than-ample evidence, primarily through his own journalistic and social media output, that Toby Young believes that dramatic levels of inequality – the opposite of 'a level playing field' – are justifiable (he has often gone on record defending the aristocracy). It is also well known, to those with enough of the relevant cultural capital, that Michael Young's 1958 bestseller *The Rise of the Meritocracy* critiqued the concept. The book was a satire, with the first half documenting the expansion of democracy in Britain, and the second imagining a sci-fi dystopia featuring a black market trade in brainy babies. The *New Republic* columnist Jeet Heer tweeted on 1 January: 'Michael Young was the great theorist of meritocracy. Toby Young is the living refutation of meritocracy'.

Toby Young's vested interests in the perpetuation of an elite, including himself, were eventually too graphic and too difficult to refute. Yet prior to his departure, vigorous attempts were made by the right to present him – just as the OFS is being presented to the public more generally – as a conduit of exactly the 'fair' social mobility that meritocracy has in recent decades been understood as involving. Even a critical piece in the *Independent* which suggested that Toby reaped what he sowed on social media presented him as an advocate for 'social mobility' and 'fair access', as a:

> [..] high profile champion of the government's Free Schools programme, who believes in social mobility and the provision of (slight traditional) standards of excellence. The new board [the OFS] exists to regulate and "uphold standards at universities" and to promote fair access to higher education, as well as safeguarding the right to free speech on campuses and preventing radicalisation.[3]

The entire incident is very revealing. It indicates how the ideology of meritocracy is put to work by the right and used by a plutocracy to try to extend its power, and what it might take to challenge it. Michael and Toby Young's different interpretations of the idea of meritocracy involve far more than dramatic differences between father and son. It indicates wider, and equally dramatic, mutations of the meaning of meritocracy itself since the 1950s. ('The idea of meritocracy may have many virtues' wrote Amartya Sen, 'but clarity is not one of them').[4] And crucially, it indicates that the expanding use of the idea of meritocracy over the past few decades has served as an extremely potent, yet highly flexible, justification for contemporary capitalist culture.

Old meritocracy

The discourse of meritocracy has multiple geographical connections and historical roots. We might trace its contemporary meaning, for instance, back to the Victorian *Self Help* narrative popularised in 1859 by Samuel Smiles, or the idea of working for consumer wealth which has been so integral to the American Dream. We might connect it to how competition is popularised as the route to diversity in contemporary Singapore; or to the advent of access to jobs by open examination in Imperial China or the nineteenth century British civil service.[5] There are many different genealogical connections, in other words, to different components of the term.

By contrast, the actual word 'meritocracy' in English is less than a hundred years old. Its first recorded use discovered to date was made by the industrial sociologist Alan Fox in 1956 in the journal *Socialist Commentary*, a weekly publication to the left of the Labour party described by former Prime Minister Clement Attlee as 'a useful corrective to the *New Statesman*'.[6] For Fox, a 'meritocracy' was unequivocally a 'grotesque' and 'ruthless' social order which divided people 'into the blessed and the unblessed – those who get the best and most of everything, and those who get the poorest and the least'. A meritocracy, according to Fox, was a society in which

> the gifted, the smart, the energetic, the ambitious and the ruthless are carefully sifted out and helped towards their destined positions of dominance, where they proceed not only to enjoy the fulfilment of exercising their natural endowments but also to receive a fat bonus thrown in for good measure.

But, he wrote:

> This is not enough. Merely to devise bigger and better 'sieves' ('equality of opportunity') to help the clever boys get to the top and then pile rewards on them when they get there is the vision is the certain brand of New Conservatism; it has never been the vision of socialism.[7]

Instead of a punitive meritocracy which rewards existing privilege, Fox suggests redistribution in economic terms and extra leisure time for those performing exceptionally dull or unattractive work, a practice he terms 'cross-grading'.

The meaning of 'meritocracy' as a set of practices being pushed by the right was understood by those on the left of the 1950s as noxious and reprehensible. In a now-forgotten review of Michael Young's *The Rise of the Meritocracy* the cultural theorist Raymond Williams (a Cambridge don, new left intellectual, and later member of Plaid Cymru) pointed out in 1958 that meritocracy had dazzled many working-class leaders and was objectionable in two respects: firstly, it weakened community and the task of common betterment; and secondly, it 'sweeten[ed] the poison of hierarchy' by offering advancement through merit rather than money or birth, whilst retaining a commitment to the very notion of hierarchy itself.[8] Meritocracy, wrote Williams, was thus 'an alternative to solidarity'.

The Rise of the Meritocracy, whilst very amusing and inventive, was less politically clear in its commitment to comprehensive socialist provision of basic services than Fox or Williams. This more liberal social democratic streak was clear in Young's later statements and activities (he joined the SDP in 1981, for instance), brilliantly imaginative though many of his projects were.[9] *The Rise of the Meritocracy* was also specifically a riposte to education policy over grammar schools, a subject which similarly concerned the philosopher Hannah Arendt, writing an article on education and meritocracy in the same year. Arendt unequivocally asserted that 'meritocracy contradicts the principle of equality, of an equalitarian democracy, no less than any other oligarchy'.[10] She discussed how the system emerging in England meant that 'even under a socialist government', the country would run as it always has done, 'as an oligarchy or aristocracy – the latter in case one takes the view that the most gifted are also the best, which is by no means a certainty'. 'Meritocracy' could certainly not be understood as egalitarian.

But by the 1970s, a liberal use of 'meritocracy' began to be pushed more firmly, and not uncoincidentally at the same time as a neoliberal politics advocating the expansion of corporate power began to take hold. Daniel Bell, who was also a friend of Michael Young's, wrote a piece arguing that meritocracy should be used as an engine of productivity for the new knowledge economy.[11] By the 1980s, meritocracy was being energetically pushed by right-wing think tanks as a justification for selling off and privatizing the provision of the welfare state. The Social Market Foundation, for example, published a pamphlet called

Meritocracy and the Classless Society which promoted educational stratification, the dismantling of the comprehensive system and the privatization of schools.[12] 'Equality of opportunity' would entail extreme hierarchies of wealth, education and status through which those with enough talent and 'grit' would be enabled to rise.

Neoliberal meritocracy

The structural and conceptual problem, of course, is that extreme inequalities of wealth are inevitable when capitalism is maximised and collectivised forms of provision are minimised. This is not an 'equal playing field' (a sporting metaphor popularised surprisingly late in the day, incidentally, by right wing management books in the 1980s). On the contrary, it means that only middle- and upper-class parents can have the resources to subsidise the intensive coaching for entrance exams and internships that are now positioned as the route to career success. Most people understand that the field is not level, and so the ideology of meritocracy is at its most vulnerable when the field is dramatically uneven, in times like the present, when eight people own as much wealth as half the world, and in the UK we have extremes of inequality not seen for a century.[13]

Neoliberal meritocracy assumed its full political force in the 1980s. Despite its huge social success building the welfare state, the Labour party was never as egalitarian and anti-meritocratic as many wanted,[14] and mid-century welfarism undoubtably privileged the patriarchy and those with white skin. Some of this resentment around social inequalities was leveraged by Thatcherism which, alongside its racism and social conservatism on questions of sexual morality, was profoundly anti-establishment in relation to class: the Thatcher government vigorously pushed a dream that anyone could make it, and linked emancipation and social mobility to the acquisition of consumer goods, home ownership and the privatisation of public utilities and social housing stock.

Blairism added a crucial new ingredient to this mix: social liberalism. New Labour promoted anti-sexism, gay rights and anti-racism. Now anyone could make it, so the story went, gay or straight, brown or white. The selective and significant provision New Labour made via SureStart (support for parents and children in deprived areas) and in tackling child poverty was far better than the family policies of Conservative governments; and yet it perpetuated the idea that, after childhood, savage individualistic competition was both fair enough and the correct way to run a society. As part of this ideology, shared by the Clintons in the US, New Labour pushed through reforms extending the process of privatising public services, through, for example, the private finance initiative (PFI) and the public-private partnerships (PPP). These initiatives handed a huge amount of power to private business interests, letting them profit from prisons and education, and helping further the shredding of social provisions by putting them in the hands of corporations.

Meritocracy within neoliberalism has had two key features that made it different from meritocracy in the past. First, it has drawn, highly selectively, on some of the energy and power of the social movements of the 1960s and 1970s, by extracting the elements that could be made compatible with capitalism: the idea that anyone, regardless of gender, ethnicity or sexual orientation, can 'make it'. Second, it has extended the idea of competitive individualism into the nooks and crannies of everyday life, through, for example, personal branding and the extension of entrepreneurial activity to the everyday. The people that did make it 'up the ladder' have been increasingly spotlighted by media narratives as parables of progress, shining examples which ordinary people needed to emulate. In neoliberal Britain, the rise of the TV talent show and thrusting business competitions boomed; business entrepreneurialism, rather than, say, lessons learned from co-operatives, were taught in schools. The problems of downward social mobility, and the question of the value and social worth of jobs at the 'top' (entrepreneur rather than nurse) were either downplayed, or mysteriously absent.

Where was Toby Young? In the early 1990s Toby Young founded the glossy libertarian *Modern Review* with professional contrarian Julie Burchill and Cosmo Landesman. Launched at the zenith of postmodernism, it aimed for highbrow writing on low culture and gleefully attempted to attack sacred cows. Its cover 'Swinging London', for example, featured a woman in a Union Jack mini dress hanging herself.[15] This was an aesthetic which embraced glamour and the contrarian spirit of punk in the service of a profoundly apolitical corporate populism which saw nothing wrong with, and did nothing whatsoever to challenge, the expansion of the market. The fusion of 'anything goes' libertarianism, 'anti-establishment' punk and the uncritical promotion of corporate values fit into the same cultural seam as the online magazine *Spiked* and Johnny Lydon selling Country Life butter. This was not just, as Anthony Barnett's handy phrase defining pro-market cultural activity under Blairism and beyond conjures up, 'corporate populism'[16]: it was also a kind of *corporate libertarianism*. Anything goes, apart from anything smelling like socialism.

Alternatives to neoliberal meritocracy

Meritocracy under neoliberalism has adopted many different guises, taking various forms and adopting different accents. But it always shares the same distinguishing feature: being used to extend plutocracy, or government by the wealthy for the wealthy. David Cameron's government perpetuated neoliberal meritocracy but made it more punitive: in the 'Aspiration Nation' it was your own fault if you failed.[17] When Theresa May came to power her first speech promised to level the playing field and release the poor, the non-white, the oppressed women from injustice.[18] What the *Sun* dubbed 'Mayritocracy' foregrounded social disadvantage, but prescribed nationalism, savage cuts to socialised provision and aid to corporations as the solution.

Like corporations using feminism in advertising, May offered what I have termed 'neoliberal justice narratives': identifying inequality and prescribing competitive capitalist solutions. Trump advocates a more volatile, extreme and overtly racist but economically similar set of policies in the US. He appeals to the idea that people should be able to make it into the US on 'merit', just like he claims to deserve the job of President on the same basis. When the social fabric is turned into a savage competition, we should not be surprised when the sons, and less occasionally daughters, of billionaires and aristocrats use their tremendous advantage to 'make it' by making desperate attempts to conserve their own privilege, from Trump all the way down to Toby Young.

Returning to the socially liberal, pro-corporate 'centre ground' will not help inequality, or climate change, or Labour's ability to connect with the profoundly disenfranchised communities a million miles away from the lifestyle lived by Toby Young. So far, Young has continued his father's commitment to try to take an 'unconventional' approach to issues, but whereas Michael Young largely channeled this through forms of social provision for all who needed it, primarily outside of corporate interests, Toby Young's approach is, as he himself readily admits, 'a capitalist' and conservative one, and his work has served to expand inequality and corporate power. In this particular case, given that his corporate libertarianism – cf. his talk of breasts and wheelchairs – is so flamboyant, the contrast with any actual commitment to equality is palpable. The contradictions of the powerful will not always be so obvious, particularly when they have such powerful media machines at their disposal.

Meritocracy has been such a powerful discourse because it reacts against inherited privilege. But at the same time it is used to marketise the idea of equality and to extend the power of plutocrats. Instead we need to return to the critique offered by Hannah Arendt, or that of Raymond Williams and Alan Fox: a socialist critique of meritocracy. This critique will only have enough power if is profoundly participatory. Since the term meritocracy appeared we have hurtled from the Fordist family wage to both sexes overworking; from sidelining differently-abled bodied to cutting the very material support they need to live; from structural racism to the inequalities of corporate multiculturalism; and through the social expansion of rampant inequality. We need to reconfigure this landscape. As a nation, we have never tried an anti-sexist, anti-racist, anti-authoritarian form of socialized provision before: and now, when we might actually have the possibility of it on the horizon, we need to do everything we can to achieve it.

Being against neoliberal meritocracy does not involve thinking that everyone can or should be a brain surgeon. 'From each according to her ability, to each according to her needs' is not a recipe for uniformity. If we value manual labour and pay it well, if we give people with unusually difficult jobs enough time off and resources to cope, if we ensure everyone has their basic needs met and the ability to flourish, life is better for everyone. Being against meritocracy needs to involve being imaginative and meaningfully democratic all the way down in order to counter fears of uniformity and the powerful ideology that competitive individualism is the only route to flourishing. This involves adopting measures towards radically reducing economic inequality (such as the high pay cap) that have been so well outlined in Andrew Sayer, Danny Dorling, Kate Pickett and Richard Wilkinson's recent work.[19] It involves funding universal public services, as Anna Coote argues, and developing forms of meaningful co-production, as fleshed out by Compass.[20] It can involve a whole host of other policies, from rent caps to placing water fountains in every public park, nationalising the railways and taking on the potential of the platform economy through an Uber run by TFL.[21] We can have inclusive comprehensive schools; we can have universities which work together. We can teach the history of co-operation and unionization. Have political parties that are meaningful at a local level. Value the social and cultural merit of working, playing and living together, rather than competing alone.

Jo Littler is Reader in the Sociology Department at City, University of London and a member of the editorial collective of *Soundings: A Journal of Politics and Culture*. Her new book *Against Meritocracy: Culture, Power and Myths of Mobility* is published by Routledge.

Notes

1 L. Finlayson, 'Bigger problems than Toby Young', LRB Blog, 2.1.18, https://www.lrb.co.uk/blog/2018/01/02/lorna-finlayson/bigger-problems-than-toby-young/; 'UK Higher education and the perils of 'it'll never happen', Punkacadamic, anonymous academic blog, 3.1.18, https://punkacademic.net/.

2 R. Booth 'Toby Young: social media self-obsessive still battling with his father's shadow', *Guardian*, 5.1.18, https://www.theguardian.com/media/2018/jan/05/why-impulsive-vain-toby-young-wants-us-to-take-him-seriously.

3 O. English, 'I knew Toby Young long before his appointment to the Office For Students. He was trying to erase his history even then', *Independent*, 9.1.18, http://www.independent.co.uk/voices/toby-young-university-regulator-resignation-office-for-students-what-like-before-appointment-erase-a8149476.html.

4 A. Sen, 'Merit and Justice', in K. Arrow, S. Bowles & S. Durlauf, eds, *Meritocracy and Economic Inequality*, New Jersey: Princeton University Press, 2000, p7.

5 B. A. Elman, *Civil Examinations and Meritocracy in Late Imperial China,* Cambridge, Harvard University Press, 2013; N. Talib & R. Fitzgerald, 'Inequality as Meritocracy: The use of the metaphor of diversity and the value of inequality within Singapore's meritocratic education system', *Critical Discourse Studies,* 2015.

6 R. M. Douglas, 'No Friend of Democracy: The Socialist Vanguard Group 1941-50', *Contemporary British History*, 2002.

7 A. Fox, 'Class and Equality', *Socialist Commentary*, May 1956, p13.

8 R. Williams, 'Democracy or Meritocracy?' *Manchester Guardian,* 30.10.58, p10.

9 Young quoted in G, Dench, ed, *The Rise and Rise of Meritocracy*, Oxford, Wiley-Blackwell, 2006, p74. See also L. Butler, 'Michael Young, The Institute of Community Studies and the Politics of Kinship', *Twentieth Century British History*, 2015.

10 H. Arendt, 'The Crisis in Education', *Partisan Review*, 1968.

11 D. Bell, 'On meritocracy and equality', *The Public Interest*, Fall 1972.

12 A. Wooldridge, *Meritocracy and the 'Classless Society',* London: Social Market Foundation, 1995.

13 D. Hardoon, *An Economy for the 99%,* London, Oxfam, 2017. See also T. Piketty, et al, *World Inequality Report 2018,* http://wir2018.wid.world/.

14 S. Todd, *The People: The Rise and Fall of the Working Class, 1910-2010,* London: John Murray, 2015.

15 *The Modern Review*, 1.10.97.

16 A. Barnett, 'Corporate populism and partyless democracy', in A. Chadwick & R. Hefferman, eds, *The New Labour Reader*, Oxford: Polity, 2003.

17 For a fuller analysis see Littler, *Against Meritocracy: Culture, power and myths of mobility,* London: Routledge, 2017, pp.89-92.

18 'Theresa May's first speech to the nation as Prime Minister – in full', *Independent,* 13.7.16, http://www.independent.co.uk/news/uk/politics/theresa-mays-first-speech-to-the-nation-as-prime-minister-in-full-a7135301.html.

19 R. Wilkinson & K. Pickett, *The Spirit Level: Why Equality is Better for Everyone,* London, Penguin, 2010; A. Sayer, *Why we can't afford the rich*, Bristol: Policy Press, 2016; D. Dorling, *The Equality Effect: Improving Life for Everyone*, London: New Internationalist, 2017.

20 A. Coote, 'Are Universal Public Services the answer to Europe's widening inequalities'? Brave New Europe, 4.12.17, https://braveneweurope.com/anna-coote-are-universal-public-services-the-answer-to-europes-widening-inequalities; Z.

Gannon & N. Lawson, *Co-production: The modernisation of public services for staff and users*, London: Compass, 2008.

21 'New Economics Foundation calls for Khan's Cars as mutually owned alternative to Uber', NEF Press Release, 22.9.17, http://neweconomics.org/2017/09/new-economics-foundation-calls-khans-cars-mutually-owned-alternative-uber/.

Narrating the economy

Christine Berry

What is the story of the economy in Britain? Who gets to shape public opinion about what it's for, how it's broken and how it can be fixed? And how can progressive forces tell a new story to help accelerate the shift to a new economic system?

These are the questions the Framing the Economy project – a partnership between the New Economy Organisers' Network, the Public Interest Research Centre, the Frameworks Institute and the New Economics Foundation – set out to answer. We wanted to help civil society communicate and organise more effectively, to help bring about the changes needed to move to a sustainable, equitable and democratic economy.

Shifting sands – the context we're working in

The dominant story told about the UK economy, and the politics of that story, have changed repeatedly in the past three years. From 2010-2015, the defining story of British politics – the one that gave many progressives a rude awakening to the power of narrative – was the austerity story. The airwaves were full of politicians repeating that we had maxed out the nation's credit card and needed to stop borrowing; that the Labour government had spent too much and crashed the economy; that without drastic cuts to public spending, the UK could end up like Greece.

This story was remarkably resilient - against sluggish economic performance and failure on its own deficit reduction measures; against the reasoned arguments of Keynesian commentators; against the anger of anti-cuts campaigners. It not only reinforced austerity politics but crowded out space to talk about real threats to our economy, like climate change. It spread the feeling that sustainability and social justice were luxuries the UK could no longer afford.

At the same time, George Lakoff's book *Don't Think of an Elephant!*[1] was popularising the idea that the way we frame issues radically shapes the way people think about them. Many on the left became increasingly convinced that our tactics needed a radical rethink – that trying to combat a simple and powerful story with facts, statistics, myth-busters and appeals to fairness was doomed to fail. As one senior press officer put it to us, 'We brought a spreadsheet to a knife fight.' More fundamentally, many began to suspect that our efforts to rebut the austerity story were actually reinforcing its boundaries – that we were playing into the hands of our opponents, and urgently needed to tell a new story of our own. It was against this backdrop that Framing the Economy was conceived.

In the years since then, British politics has been turned upside down. Over the past two years, the meetings of the Framing the Economy Network – a group of 40 top progressive communicators and campaigners who have been part of the project – have sometimes felt like group therapy. Brexit, Theresa May becoming Prime Minister, Trump becoming President, the shock 2017 election results – each of our meetings seemed to be accompanied by a new political earthquake. It was easy to feel bewildered, politically jet-lagged, struggling to remould our assumptions around an ever-changing reality. But it was also a huge privilege to be able to navigate this increasingly unpredictable world with such an impressive, committed and diverse group of people.

In 2016, a new story took hold of the public debate: the Brexit story. The Leave campaign insisted that the UK needed to 'take back control' from distant elites in Brussels, that our economy would thrive if only we could make our own decisions. This proved an immensely powerful story for millions of people who felt ignored and disenfranchised. (Though of course, many comfortably-off people in the south east and elsewhere also voted for Leave.) But of course, the Brexit story is not only a story about elites, but about outsiders of all kinds: it has gone hand in hand with the demonization of migrants and a terrifying rise in racism and xenophobia.

In 2017, we saw a glimpse of what could happen if the British people were offered a more positive story about our collective future. Against virtually all expert predictions, Jeremy Corbyn's Labour Party came to the brink of power with a message of ending austerity, rebuilding the public sphere and reclaiming common ownership of resources like energy and the railways. Ideas which had been taboo for a generation were suddenly back on the political agenda.

It is not only the content of these stories that has shifted the context we are working in, but also the way they have taken hold. During the Brexit campaign, economic experts lined up to warn of dire consequences to the UK economy if we voted to leave the EU. This was not only ineffective, but even seems to have strengthened the anti-establishment credentials of the Leave campaign. This challenges the widely-held assumption that the austerity story was powerful partly because it was presented as the expert economic consensus. Meanwhile, the 2017 election demonstrated the power of both grassroots organising and social media to mobilise people and upend the political consensus. The mainstream media may have been telling one story, but people's votes told quite another.

This forces us to think again about what it means to shift the narrative, and to be much more imaginative about the channels through which we try and do this. This is challenging, but also exciting: if the battlefield is indeed shifting from the difficult terrain of the elite media discourse to Labour's more natural territory of the doorstep (and – hopefully a strength for Labour – the Facebook page), this surely presents a huge opportunity for the left to fight on stronger ground.

Understanding how people think

To navigate these shifting sands successfully, we need to give ourselves a firm foundation. Beneath the tumult and upheaval, what are the shared assumptions – the durable 'cultural models' – that organise and shape people's thinking about the economy? Which of these can be leveraged productively to support new thinking, and which do we need to avoid or counter? We investigated this via 40 interviews with a demographically diverse sample of people from across the UK.

The cognitive hole

The first and perhaps most striking finding was how few models people have available to help them think about the economy. The economy is intimidating. Most people struggled to answer questions about how they thought the economy worked, and the models they did draw on provided only the sketchiest accounts of the actual *mechanisms* that structure economic outcomes. This is unsurprising: previous research has found that only around a third of British people feel comfortable engaging with economics,[2] only 17% think they have a good understanding of how big businesses work,[3] and most could not accurately define key economic concepts like GDP[4] and the deficit.[5]

This 'cognitive hole' presents a challenge for progressive communicators, but also an opportunity. The challenge is that our communications about the economy have a very thin base to build on: there's a lot of work to do if we want to help people join the dots between different economic issues and progressive solutions, and feel empowered to act. Just think of the housing crisis as an example: how can we translate the complex problems of financialisation, privatisation and rent extraction into a story that points towards real solutions, that rejects the simplistic mantras of 'build more homes' or 'stop housing immigrants', but that is empowering rather than overwhelming?

The opportunity lies in the fact that we aren't up against a solid, well-constructed neoliberal account of the economy that people draw on consistently to explain why things work the way they do. People may have internalised aspects of neoliberal ideology – such as the idea that people are inherently greedy, that the economy is synonymous with money, or that competition is inevitable, all of which came through strongly in our interviews – but these are piecemeal and sporadic: they do not add up to a coherent model of how the economy works that needs to be dismantled. (Again, this chimes with the findings of previous polling that the British public never fully bought into the dogma of privatisation, with large majorities consistently favouring public ownership.)

At one level, this may mean that progressives can cut through the public debate and begin to shift its terms with relatively straightforward and simple frames. But the deeper prize here goes beyond communications itself. Through grassroots public education initiatives, integrated with campaigns, political movements and community projects, we can begin to empower people so that they *do* feel the economy is something they have the right to an opinion on, something they are confident talking about, and not just an intimidating black box that only experts can understand.

Who's pulling the strings?

In some cases, this 'cognitive hole' was linked to a belief that the economy is simply a force of nature that cannot really be understood or controlled – rather than a system constructed by humans that can be rebuilt by humans. As one focus group participant put it, 'You can't redesign something that wasn't designed in the first place.' But our interviews also revealed a powerful and consistent sense that 'the system is rigged': that the economy works the way it does because powerful elites have structured it to serve their interests. Many on the left would argue that this instinct is essentially accurate – that reshaping the economy around the interests of economic elites has been at the heart of the neoliberal project, from deregulating the banks to enabling landlords to exploit tenants. Perhaps tapping into this instinctive understanding could provide a starting point for a compelling story about what needs to change.

The problem is that, without a clear understanding of *how* and *why* this has happened, this model is much less useful for the left than we might assume. Firstly, it tended to lead people to focus on the actions of 'bad apples' rather than on how the system needs to change – on nefarious individuals rather than broken structures. Second, the idea that these elites have almost complete control over what happens made people deeply fatalistic about the possibility of changing the economy. When asked about how the economy could be different, most of our interviewees found it almost impossible to imagine alternatives. While this no doubt reflects the left's failure to develop and articulate alternatives, it is also a logical result of the dominant cultural models at play.

Finally, people tended to conflate economic elites with political elites – so rather than seeing democratic control as a way of curtailing elite power, government potentially becomes part of the problem. (It's worth noting that interviewees consistently felt that government was responsible for solving economic problems – they just may not trust it to do so.) As one interviewee put it: 'I think politicians forget that we live on one planet and it's all about their own greed. I think the economy is set by men in suits basically and they will always profit from it, and profit enormously.'

The success of right-wing populists like Nigel Farage at co-opting anti-elitist rhetoric for regressive ends has left many progressives bewildered and angry. But on this evidence, perhaps we should not be so surprised. To build a compelling case for change, we need to do more than simply stoke people's anger at elites. We need to situate this within a wider story that explains *how* this has come to pass and how, by acting together, we can build something different and better.

Telling new stories

In the second phase of our work, Framing the Economy set out to find the building blocks of such a story. We used a range of methods including 'on-the-street' interviews (think vox pop with framing), focus groups and a large-scale survey experiment (6,600 respondents) to test how different values, metaphors and examples affected people's thinking about the economy. Our outcome measures included support for progressive economic policies, but also things like who people blamed for economic problems, how far they thought of the economy as the product of human design, and how optimistic they felt that the economy could be improved by our collective efforts.

In doing this, we had in mind a very live debate between two different types of story: what I think of as the 'take back control' story and the 'all of us first' story. The 'take back control' story is exemplified by Jeremy Corbyn's left populist relaunch, under the retro slogan 'for the many, not the few'. Corbyn's recent face-off with Morgan Stanley – 'when they say we're a threat, they're right. We're a threat to a damaging and failed system that's rigged for the few' – is perhaps the purest expression of this story in action.[6] The thinking behind this story is that the anti-establishment rage being harnessed by the far-right is something that properly belongs to the left – that taking on elites is our job, and only by credibly promising to do it can we successfully take on right-wing populism. This sometimes goes along with an argument that only by pointing the finger at a new 'enemy' can we deflect the blame currently being directed at immigrants and benefit claimants.

The 'all of us first' story is exemplified by the work of Common Weal to build a positive progressive vision for Scotland. Their manifesto for change characterises neoliberalism as 'me-first politics' and contrasts this with a politics that puts 'all of us first'. Advocates of this story argue that countering neoliberalism with a populist story that pits 'us' against 'them' is like trying to fight fire with fire. It's only by telling stories that unify, that testify to our ability to achieve more by working together than we can by fighting each other, that we can hope to overturn a neoliberal story that emphasises competition and individualism. We should focus on the world we want to build and the lives we want to lead, not the people we want to take on. Some also worry that stoking a politics of blame will ultimately exacerbate racism and xenophobia rather than deflecting it: after all, history shows that hating economic elites and hating immigrants are far from mutually exclusive.

What our research suggests is that both of these stories can be effective – although only when used in certain ways, and probably not at the same time.

The populist story: taking back control

Let's take the first story – which we've characterised in our recommendations as 'the populist story'. Our survey experiment found that messages which combined an explanation of how neoliberal policy has empowered elites with the values of equality (elite capture is making our economy unequal when it should be fair to everyone) or economic strength (elite capture is undermining the strength of our economy so it doesn't work well) produced a significant rise in support for a range of progressive policies. The value of economic strength seemed particularly effective at shifting attitudes among Conservative voters.

Separately, we tested a metaphor of 'reprogramming the economy', comparing the economy to a computer program to which elites have gained the password, so ordinary people are 'locked out'. This significantly enhanced people's perception that the economy was designed by people, that we could and should act together to redesign it, and that policy had a role to play in shaping these outcomes. Given that people tend to see the economy as a 'black box', metaphors are useful because they invite comparison with something more familiar – demystifying the economy and providing a frame for thinking about how it works. We think that combining these various 'frame elements' into a coherent story about how we can redistribute power away from elites has real potential to open up new ways of thinking about the economy, without inadvertently reinforcing fatalism or anti-government sentiment.

The common ground story: all of us first

The second story, which we've characterised as the 'common ground' story, is built on the value of fulfilment. We found that engaging this value also significantly boosted support for progressive policy, but that it behaved in the opposite way to the values of equality and economic strength. Where the latter two values only seemed to be effective when coupled with a story about elite capture, fulfilment was only effective when *not* coupled with this story. We think this is because these two frames reflect two different types of argument. Where the populist story is essentially a story about power – who has it, why this is bad and how it needs to be redistributed – the common ground story is essentially a story about priorities. It argues that the economy isn't meeting our real needs – *anyone's* real needs; that we need to look not only at how money is distributed but also at what we want that money *for*. We think this story taps into a deep sense that our society has the wrong priorities: that things like community, safety and time to enjoy life are more important than chasing growth and profits.

With this story, we recommend using a metaphor that compares the economy to a network of railway tracks. This metaphor can be used in a variety of ways – to talk about how the economy isn't taking us to the places we really want to go, or about how we've built tracks that are only serving some parts of the country while leaving others stranded. The key thing is that people built the tracks and people can remake them to better serve our needs. Like the 'reprogramming' metaphor, we found that this significantly boosted people's sense that the economy was designed and could be redesigned. However, it lends itself less to talking about imbalances of power and more to talking about the 'destination': the needs which economic activity should help everyone up and down the country to fulfil.

With everything we tested, we were careful to avoid language that could play into a narrow or exclusive concept of the British nation, and found no evidence that these messages encouraged people to blame immigrants or those at the bottom for economic problems (though it's worth noting that we also didn't find compelling evidence they made this *less* likely, as some have suggested).

What next?

Of course, this is far from the end of the story. We have already begun work with campaigners on different single issues, from housing to deregulation, to explore how these general findings might apply to their work – and we hope to do much more. We also have plans to shift focus from building a compelling story to building the infrastructure the left needs to tell that story well – from training our press officers to sharing best practice and latest research. And doing this work has left us more convinced than ever that efforts to shift the narrative must fill not just a communications gap, but an intellectual gap and an organising gap. We need new ideas, new solutions and new ways of making them a reality just as much as we need new messages.

These are times of great possibility and also of great danger. For the first time in decades, there is a sense that the economic consensus is fracturing, that a change must and will come. A space has opened up to talk and think differently about the economy. The question is what this space will be filled by: a narrow, nationalistic story which scapegoats outsiders, or a positive vision for a just and sustainable future? It is imperative that civil society rises to the challenge. We hope that Framing the Economy provides a solid foundation for this vital task – but the real work is only just beginning.

For those wishing to learn more either about the findings or about methodology, the full report of the Framing the Economy project is available at http://neweconomyorganisers.org/our-work/framing-the-economy/.

Christine Berry is a Doctoral Researcher at Sheffield Political Economy Research Institute, and a member of the Framing the Economy Project. She was previously Principal Director for Policy & Government at NEF.

Notes

1 G.Lakoff, *Don't think of an elephant! Know your values and frame the debate,* London: Chelsea Green Publishing, 2004.

2 YouGov / Post Crash Economics Society, 2015, https://d25d2506sfb94s.cloudfront.net/cumulus_uploads/document/1hodojy30j/PostCrashEconomicsSocietyResults_150128_economics_W.pdf.

3 Populus, 2015, 'The Multiple Faces of Corporate Reputation', http://s3.amazonaws.com/wavecast-production/wavecast-platform/sites/277/2015/07/The-Multiple-Faces-of-Corporate-Reputation-Report_28.07.15.pdf.

4 YouGov / Rethinking Economics, 2015.

5 YouGov / Sun on Sunday, 2015, https://d25d2506sfb94s.cloudfront.net/cumulus_uploads/document/2rm330ydgm/SOS_Results_150115_Website.pdf.

6 R.Mason, 'Jeremy Corbyn tells Morgan Stanley, You're right, we are a threat', *Guardian,* 30.11.17, https://www.theguardian.com/politics/2017/nov/30/jeremy-corbyn-morgan-stanley-labour-brexit.

Feminism and the Labour Left: a perfect political union?

Charlotte Proudman

Socialist and feminist politics have sometimes had a difficult relationship in the past, but an intersectional approach can move past these issues. This article looks at the importance of culture and policy, and sets out four ways feminist policies should feature in Labour's programme for 2018 and beyond.

Socialist politics has sometimes had a difficult relationship with issues of gender inequality and feminism, but, since at least the 1980s, the Labour Party has committed itself to championing gender equality alongside issues of class and economic equality. This article examines the relationship between socialism, Labour, the Labour Left and feminism historically, before turning to key feminist policies and debates in the present, in order to suggest how gender should feature in Labour's programme for 2018 and beyond.

Socialism and feminism have the potential to be reconciled. The theory of 'intersectionality', an idea coined by Kimberle Crenshaw in the 1980s, offers a way forward. Applying an intersectional approach involves identifying the different strands of people's experiences and vectors of identity and oppression stemming from gender, race, class, disability, religion and immigration status. This has yet to become mainstream within political parties, but it is vital for Labour to take intersectionality seriously if we are to deal effectively with all the facets of inequality in twenty-first century Britain.

Socialism and feminism in history

Marxism and feminism have often occupied a tense and uncomfortable position alongside each other in politics. Some feminists contend that marxism is inherently masculine, pursuing the interests of the white, male working class and focusing on class inequality to the exclusion of gender inequality. According to lawyer and feminist legal scholar Catherine MacKinnon, marxism focused on how the state manifests class power and inequality and how a class-based society can be transformed.[1] It offers little space for thinking about gender as a distinct axis of inequality and oppression. MacKinnon succinctly sums up the divergence between feminism and marxism: 'sexuality is to feminism what work is to marxism: that which is most one's own yet most taken away.'[2] Feminism and marxism, in this reading, have fundamentally different priorities.

Women were also generally marginalised from radical and liberal politics in the nineteenth century. The Chartists famously demanded universal *manhood* suffrage in the 1840s. And MacKinnon highlighted the fact that liberal thinker John Stuart Mill's famous petition in Parliament in 1866 for women's suffrage was partially justified on the basis that 'the majority of women of any class are not likely to differ in political opinion from the majority of men in the same class.'[3] The class of a woman's husband often determined her position in society. Gender inequality has not always been at the heart of left politics.

The traditional focus of the Labour Party in the early and mid-twentieth century was often on 'labourist' issues, neglecting women's and ethnic minorities' roles in society. Men and class were prioritised over women, gender and other vectors of inequality. This stemmed partly from the socialist ideologies that shaped the early Labour Party, and, even more so, from the significance of trade unionism to the party. The trade union movement has historically represented a particular sub-section of society: broadly, white working-class men who are union members, and who are particularly likely to be in stable, skilled or semi-skilled manual work. The visibility of women at the top of trade unions is woefully lacking, even though we now have our first female TUC general secretary, Frances O'Grady. In the many years she has worked for the TUC, O'Grady has consistently aimed to challenge the 'male, pale and stale' stereotype and shift the movement 'to a profile that better fits a six million plus membership that is now 50:50 men and women'.[4] Trade unions are, however, still largely controlled and dominated by white men. The lack of women in leadership roles will inevitably impact upon the prioritisation of women's workplace issues, such as gender discrimination and sexual harassment.

It took collective action from women within the Labour Party and labour movement more broadly from the 1960s to the 1990s to demand that gender inequality was put firmly on the Party's agenda. Eventually all-women shortlists were introduced at the 1993 Labour Party conference, and a record number of Labour women MPs were elected in 1997 under Tony Blair's leadership. This initiative was a move from the centre of the Party. Yet many on the Labour Left had also championed gender equality and the representation of women in politics in the 1980s: in local government, Labour in places like Sheffield and the Greater London Council created women's committees, gave grants to feminist organisations, and fought for gender equality. This inheritance must be built on today.

Prostitution: a flashpoint issue

In recent years, the leadership of the Labour Party and some trade unions have championed the full decriminalisation of prostitution. This would allow men the right to use their capital to buy women's bodies; those bodies would become *just* another mode of production in the free market. Prostitution is a gendered issue: approximately 80,000 people, mostly women, are prostitutes in Britain, and the majority of buyers are men.[5] The gendered dynamic of prostitution is lost on Aslef, however, a British trade union for train drivers, whose membership base comprises of 20,287 men and 1,067 women, and which backed a motion for the decriminalisation of prostitution, which was put to a vote at the TUC Congress.[6] Former deputy Labour leader and feminist Harriet Harman intervened in the debate and condemned the move arguing it would 'legitimise their exploitation'.[7] Delegates voted overwhelmingly against the motion.

Jeremy Corbyn and John McDonnell have both also supported decriminalisation; both have a long history of supporting the English Collective of Prostitutes, a campaign group that seeks the decriminalisation of prostitution. At

Goldsmiths University in 2016, Corbyn said, 'I am in favour of decriminalising the sex industry. I don't want people to be criminalised. I want to be [in] a society where we don't automatically criminalise people. Let's do things a bit differently and in a bit more civilised way'.[8] He does not support the criminalisation of men who buy sex (the 'Sex Buyer Law') either.

While the criminalisation of women who work as prostitutes further victimises them, calls for full decriminalisation imply that the purchase of women's bodies can be civilised. This is a highly questionable claim: statistics show over 50 per cent of prostituted women in the UK started being paid for sex acts before they were 18[9]; over 50 per cent prostituted women have been raped and/sexually assaulted;[10] 9 of 10 prostituted women report wanting to exit prostitution but feel unable to.[11] In Germany, where prostitution is legal, the consequence is increased demand and soaring supply. Prostitutes can be hired in a similar way to hiring an uber and 99 euros buys access to King George Brothel where it is possible to have sex with as many women as are available and the drinks are included.[12] Sex in a context of inequality – payment for a woman's body – is unequal and consent cannot make it equal. In 2014, the European Parliament passed a non-binding resolution in favour of criminalising the purchase of sex because it reinforces the objectification of women and sustains prostitution.[13]

How have some trade unions and the leadership of the Labour Party got the issue of prostitution so wrong? We can trace their views back to early Marxists and socialists' assumptions about class, capitalism and work. Marx himself stated that 'prostitution is only a *specific* expression of the *general* prostitution of the *labourer*'.[14] Marx believed prostitution simply represented the exploitation and degradation of wage labour. Selma James, a supporter of Jeremy Corbyn and the first spokesperson of the English Collective of Prostitutes, argued that women's work, whether outside the home, in the home, or in the bedroom, should be compensated with a wage (hence her most well-known campaign, 'Wages for Housework').

The Left of the Labour Party, the English Collective of Prostitutes, and some trade unions are working to monetise and unionise all 'work' (ironically a capitalist and libertarian argument), without recognising the intersections of structural inequality that underpin prostitution. Rather than seeking to include prostitution within a capitalist framework of 'labour', efforts should focus on eliminating an industry that is designed to exploit women in often vulnerable positions. Without an intersectional approach to understanding issues that affect minority and disadvantaged groups in society, the left appears to apply a monolithic trade union and labour-based approach to all issues. Work does not *always* liberate people.

Of course, prostitution remains a relatively marginal issue in British politics. But examining it points to conclusions about how gender fits into Corbyn's political project. It is telling that in July 2015, when Jeremy Corbyn first stood as leader of the Labour Party, he produced a six page manifesto, 'Working with Women', which stated that his aim is to 'achieve equal and better pay for all, and support career progression for all women through better trade union recognition and collective bargaining'.[15] But feminist issues cannot be subsumed into class inequality. Labour needs to recognise this.

Gender and feminist issues in Corbyn's politics

The Labour Left argues, with some justification that Corbyn's anti-austerity strategy speaks to women's needs, since women have been the main targets and victims of Tory austerity policies.[16] By prioritising the public sector, in particular the NHS, education and social welfare, which employ many women and which women are more likely to rely upon, Labour argues that it is ensuring women's needs are met. But this still focuses on work and economics.

Second wave feminists sought to make the private political. As critical theorist and feminist Nancy Fraser states, feminism 'rightly criticised the constricted political vision that was so intently focused on class inequality that it could not see such "non-economic" injustices as domestic violence, sexual assault and reproductive oppression'.[17] Under Corbyn's leadership, Labour needs to take more seriously these 'non-economic' injustices. In 2016, when Jeremy Corbyn stood for a second time as leader of the party, he produced a 10 point manifesto 'to rebuild and transform Britain', but there was no specific point relating to women: rather women were shoehorned into education and securing an equal society.[18] Labour's 2017 General Election manifesto was widely popular, but paid scant attention to gender inequality.[19] The party needs to do better.

One policy floated by Jeremy Corbyn in 2016 caught the attention of the public: the introduction of women-only, or gender segregated, train carriages to reduce sexual harassment by men towards women. The policy was met with public ridicule. Critics contend that it is a throw-back to the 1970s that is symptomatic of Jeremy Corbyn's understanding of gender politics. In fact it is a policy that has roots in the late nineteenth century. Women-only train carriages were introduced in 1874 by the Metropolitan Railway and officially abolished by British Rail in 1977. This policy proposal puts the onus on women's behaviour, encouraging them to sit in segregated train carriages because of a belief that some men will always sexually harass women, just as some anti-rape strategies place the onus on women's behaviour, as women are told to dress modestly, to drink responsibly and to return home at a sensible hour because some men will always rape. The emphasis is on women's behaviour: what women *could* and *should do* to prevent men from abusing them. Instead the focus should be on perpetrators of sexual assault and harassment and their behaviour towards women.

Gender segregation is a much debated issue in feminist theory. Feminist scholar Andrea Dworkin contends that mainly right-wing women and men legitimize gender segregation under the 'separate-but-equal model'.[20] This model justifies the perpetuation of the subordination of women to men by suggesting that the genders are inherently different. In the case of train carriages, men and women ride separately, yet each is doing equally what is appropriate to their gender. In the case of prostitution, according to Dworkin, the sexual subordination of women to men is seen to be in the nature of things and a logical premise of social organization. The left needs to reject all understandings of gender based on a 'separate-but-equal' model.

There are many policy proposals that Labour could adopt to demonstrate a commitment to tackling gender inequality in an intersectional way. I will share *just* a few preliminary ideas of potential changes to domestic policy.

The sex buyer law: Eliminating prostitution

The introduction of the Sex Buyer Law for prostitution, which criminalises buyers of sex, de-criminalises prostituted women and ensures state investment for women exiting prostitution. Failure to end the demand for prostitution signals a failure of the state to end violence against women (see above for the statistics of violence against prostituted women). The Sex Buyer Law has been adopted in Northern Ireland, Ireland, France, Canada, Iceland, Norway and Sweden. Sweden was the first country to introduce the law in 1997 and subsequent research has shown that:

- Street prostitution halved between 1999 and 2008 and there is no evidence women were simply displaced to indoor prostitution or prostitution was advertised online.[21]
- The number of men paying for sex in Sweden declined. In 1996, 13.6 per cent of men reported buying sex by 2008 this figure reduced to 7.9 per cent.[22]
- Public attitudes have changed towards the law. In 1996, 45 per cent women and 20 per cent men supported criminalising sex buyers by 2008, 79 per cent women and 60 per cent men were in favour of the law.[23]
- According to the National Criminal Police, Sweden has become a more hostile destination for traffickers.[24]

Prostitution disproportionately impacts upon the lives of vulnerable and marginalised women whom are exploited under conditions of sex inequality. The Labour party is a political party that strives to create a more equal society. In a gender equal society, prostitution would be an issue confined to history books. To achieve the elimination of the sex industry, the Labour party must adopt to Sex Buyer Law. It is the only law that has evidenced a marked reduction of prostitution and thus safety for women.

Quotas for women

Quotas for women in male-dominated professions, which includes but is not limited to Members of Parliament, the judiciary and the boardroom. The Labour party is the only political party to champion all-women shortlists for Members of Parliament and consequently the Labour party has the greatest number of women in parliament. An effective democracy requires the representation of a cross-section of society rather than one demographic background. Britain has failed to introduce gender quotas in any public sphere. The dogmatic argument is: we live in a meritocratic society, and if you work hard, you will succeed. However, the Labour party understands better than any other party that structural inequality means people are not competing on an equal playing field. Privileged white men have an advantage over others in terms of their capital, gender and race, which has led to them being disproportionately represented where power is wielded.

Gender quotas ensure the redistribution of male power, which is a core principle of feminism. Since Norway, Iceland, Finland and Sweden's introduced a law on quotas for women in boardrooms, these countries have nearly doubled the average percentage of women on boards to around 34 per cent, which is a stark contrast to countries without quotas in place (at about 18 per cent).[25] I am a strong advocate of quotas for women in the judiciary. Government judicial diversity statistics in 2017[26] show that women comprise only 28 per cent of all court judges, 24 per cent of Court of Appeal judges and 22 per cent of High Court judges, which is consistent with 2016. The gender imbalance between male and female judges in the UK is amongst the worst in Europe. Gender quotas in the judiciary have been tried and tested, having been introduced in the International Criminal Court, the European Court of Human Rights and the Belgium Constitutional Court, which ensures a more equal gender balance in the judiciary.[27] Should the Labour Party attain political office, Baroness Shami Chakrabarti would become the Attorney General and gender quotas could firmly be on the agenda. In her book, *Of Women: In the 21st Century* Chakrabarti[28] sets out a compelling argument for quotas in the judiciary as well as other fields.

A radical transformation of rape law.

Britain's rape laws are not working. Approximately 85,000 women are raped in England and Wales every year, that's around 11 rapes of adults every hour; only around 15 per cent of those who experience sexual violent report to the police;[29] conviction rates for rape are far lower than other crimes with only 5.7 per cent of reported rape cases ending in a conviction[30]; and only around 57.9 per cent of rape prosecutions result in a conviction.[31] Women are often reluctant to report cases of rape, given that during investigations and at trial women's sexual history is put under the microscope; women are expected to relive intimate and often traumatic memories before non-medical professionals; and they are often at the mercy of an under-resourced CPS and police force who are expected to present a robust case.

To prove rape, it must be shown beyond reasonable doubt that the defendant did not have a reasonable belief that the complainant was consenting to penetration. Consent means 'if she agrees by choice, and has the freedom and capacity to make that choice'.[32] But how can a woman be free when she is not equal? MacKinnon[33] proposes a radical transformation of existing rape laws. At present there is a presumption that if sex happened, the woman consented to it unless the prosecution proves she did not. MacKinnon argues that even if there is consent that does not make sex equal, mutual or welcome but it can make it tolerated. Just because a woman allowed sex to happen to her under the threat of being arrested or losing her job or being deported, it does not mean that she *wanted* it. It means a man exerted institutional power over her. Yet this is consensual sex according to the criminal law. MacKinnon explains that coercive submission can merge with consent because threatening conditions are a normal feature of gender relations under conditions of inequality so much so that they appear as sex.

MacKinnon proposes redefining rape laws by assessing the circumstances of inequality. This starts from a premise that rape is a crime of inequality that includes gender amongst other inequalities.[34] Consent as it's currently defined in law should be only one facet of analysis. The law should take into account inequality – such an analysis starts with the interactions and power base of the defendant in contrast to the complainant. This would involve an analysis of the hierarchal power relations of the complainant and defendant and consideration of whether the sex was welcomed, desired and based on mutuality. The larger structures of inequality in which accuser and accused are imbricated should be taken into account; men should not be able to ignore these broader power relations. Using one's power to put someone in a position where they agree to a sexual act should not be acceptable.

Universal childcare and paternity leave

Universal childcare is a policy championed by the Labour Party. At the party's annual conference in 2017, shadow Education Secretary Angela Raynor committed to universal childcare for two to four year olds for up to 30 hours a week regardless of family income for 38 weeks of the year.[35] While this is a progressive policy, it does not go far enough to assist women, who largely remain responsible for the bulk of childcare and as a consequence often forgo career advancement. Labour should commit to funding childcare from birth to school age for up to 35 hours a week for 50 weeks of the year, and upon the child reaching school age, the party should commit to funding after school childcare.

Not enough fathers opt to take paternity leave. Currently the government ensures one or two weeks paid paternity leave for fathers, which frankly is appalling and certainly does little to encourage men to parent their children in the same way mothers are expected to. The UK is lagging behind countries that champion gender equality with innovative paternity policies.[36] In Sweden, fathers receive 90 days paid paternity leave, which cannot be transferred to the mother. In Iceland, parents can split their nine months post-birth parental leave in half. Mothers are allocated three months and fathers are allocated three months. It is left to the parents to decide how to divide the remaining three months. Neither parent can transfer their three months of leave. The Labour party can lead the way in advocating for gender equality amongst parents by offering mothers and fathers equal and well-paid childcare leave.

Labour must build on the work of feminist scholars to put gender, as well as economic inequality at the heart of its programme. But policies are not the whole story: culture is significant too.

The culture of the Labour Left

As the 'liberation' movements of the 1960s and 1970s insisted, oppressed groups like women and black people need to organise themselves to fight their own oppression. Women must have a platform at the top of the Labour party to enable them to speak for themselves. 45 per cent of Labour MPs are women, but they are not so well represented in leadership positions. In September 2015, there was a political and media furore over the appointment of Corbyn's first shadow cabinet. During the leadership campaign Corbyn promised that half of his frontbench team would be women, in order to build 'a society where women and men exist as equals and flourish'.[37] Yet the top five positions – Leader, Deputy Leader, shadow Chancellor, shadow Home Secretary and shadow Foreign Secretary – were held by white men. The majority of women were relegated to junior ministerial positions. Corbyn was accused of 'bro-socialism'. Despite Corbyn's later efforts to ensure gender parity, the party still has a male Leader, Deputy Leader, Chancellor of the Exchequer, London mayor and General Secretary. The Labour party has never had a female leader (excepting interim leaders), Chancellor of the Exchequer or London mayoral candidate. The under-representation of women in positions of power in the Labour party will impact on where feminism is positioned on the political agenda. Given the Labour party's roots in socialism and labourism, with their masculine biases, more needs to be done.

A troublingly pervasive feature of left-wing Labour activist politics is misogynistic online abuse. It is true that abuse is a feature of politics right across the spectrum including in the Labour Party. When Yvette Cooper stood against Jeremy Corbyn in the Labour leadership election in 2015 she experienced a tirade of abuse, particularly from Jeremy Corbyn fans, including Twitter messages like, 'Labour leadership contest: Yvette Cooper appeals to family vote with childcare pledge. Stupid cow'.[38] Angela Eagle had a brick thrown through her constituency office window after challenging Jeremy Corbyn's leadership in 2016. Eventually she stood aside to make way for Owen Smith, who came under fire for sexist 'jokes', reminding us that no one part of the political spectrum has a monopoly on sexism. Misogynistic online abuse could have the effect of discouraging women from participating in Labour politics. It should be alien to all parts of the Labour Party.

Following the Harvey Weinstein scandal, many women came forward to report incidents of sexual harassment, assault and rape in politics. Bex Bailey, former member of the Labour Party's National Executive Committee, courageously told her story of being raped by a Labour party member and being dissuaded from bringing a complaint by another Labour Party member due to fears it could impact on her career prospects.[39] Allegations of sexually inappropriate conduct towards woman have been made against high profile Labour MPs, some of whom were suspended. Corbyn rightly condemned Westminster's culture of 'warped and degrading' sexual harassment, but given the huge respect for Corbyn in the party, he needs to use the influence he has, reiterating the message that sexist abuse (indeed online abuse generally) is anathema to the Labour Party's values over and over until such a time as it has been stamped out.

Human rights barrister Karon Monaghan QC has been appointed to undertake an independent investigation into how the Labour has handled complaints of sexism, discrimination and abuse, and to assess the party's procedures. It is to be hoped the investigation and concluding report will provide a frank review of much needed procedures to encourage women to report incidences of abuse. For example, how can the Labour party ensure anonymity of complainants? It is necessary that a complainant's identity remains anonymous, otherwise the fear that a complainant's identity could be leaked to the media will discourage complainants from coming forward and ensure impunity for perpetrators.

Conclusions

While the left of the Labour Party still has a long way to go to achieve gender equality, there are feminist Labour MPs who have a record of successfully lobbying across the political spectrum. This year Stella Creasy MP organised a feminist cross-party voting bloc which forced the government to back down and allow Northern Irish women access to NHS-funded abortions in England and Wales. Jess Phillips MP is organising Labour women MPs to work together to scrutinise the domestic violence bill, and social security reform for women, putting women at the centre of Labour's industrial strategy and focusing on carers. A feminist voting bloc that supports women has the potential to create tangible policy change. But these feminist issues need to be at the heart of everything the party does.

Potential and challenges lie ahead for the left of the Labour Party. If a Corbyn-led Labour party reflects upon its historically male roots, as well as its gender policies and applies an intersectional approach to its politics, the Labour party would be a force to be reckoned with. Intersectionality is a means of representing every cross section of society without excluding one group. The Labour Party has always been a party committed to eradicating inequality but inequality does not just relate to class, it encompasses gender, race, nationality, disability, religion and so much more. People want policies that relate to their experiences, and experiences of inequality are always intersectional.

Charlotte Proudman is a barrister in family law and public law at Goldsmith Chambers, Affiliated Researcher at the Department of Sociology, University of Cambridge, and has a PhD from Cambridge on the law and policy on FGM in England.

Notes

1 C.MacKinnon, 'Feminism, Marxism, Method, and the State: An Agenda for Theory', *Signs: Journal of Women in Culture and Society*, 1982.

2 C.MacKinnon, 'Feminism, Marxism, Method, and the State: Toward Feminist Jurisprudence', *Signs: Journal of Women in Culture and Society*, 1982.

3 Ibid.

4 See Frances O'Grady profile, https://www.tuc.org.uk/frances-ogrady-tuc-general-secretary.

5 *Paying the Price: A Consultation Paper on Prostitution*, Home Office, 2004.

6 'TUC leaders reject call to decriminalise prostitution', *Independent*, 13.9.17, http://www.independent.co.uk/news/uk/politics/tuc-leaders-prostitution-decriminalise-reject-call-trade-union-conference-sex-workers-a7944561.html.

7 'Harriet Harman clashes with unions at TUC conference over attempts to legalise prostitution', *Telegraph*, 12.9.17, http://www.telegraph.co.uk/news/2017/09/12/harriet-harman-clashes-unions-tuc-conference-attempts-legalise/.

8 'Jeremy Corbyn: "I favour decriminalising the sex industry"', *Guardian*, 4.3.16, https://www.theguardian.com/politics/2016/mar/04/jeremy-corbyn-decriminalise-sex-industry-prostitution.

9 *Paying the Price: A Consultation Paper on Prostitutin*', Home Office, 2004.

10 M.Hester & N.Westmarland, *Tackling Street Prostitution: Towards an Holistic Approach*, Home Office, London, 2004.

11 M.Farley, 'Prostitution and Trafficking in Nine Countries: An Update on Violence and Posttraumatic Stress Disorder', *Journal of Trauma Practice*, 2003.

12 Feargus O'Sullivan, ;Now You Can Hire a Prostitute Like You Hire an Uber', CityLab, 22.4.14, https://www.citylab.com/life/2014/04/now-you-can-hire-prostitute-you-hire-uber/8941/; Conor Creighton, 'A Visit to One of Germany's All-You-Can-Fuck Brothels', Vice, 16.7.14, https://www.vice.com/sv/article/mvb49p/a-visit-to-one-of-germanys-all-you-can-fuck-brothels-432.

13 'Punish the client, not the prostitute', European Parliament press release, 26.2.14, http://www.europarl.europa.eu/news/en/press-room/20140221IPR36644/punish-the-client-not-the-prostitute.

14 K.Marx, *Economic and Philosophic Manuscript of 1844*, ed. D.J.Struik, New York, International Publishers, 1964, p.133, footnote.

15 J.Corbyn, *Working with women*, 18.7.15, p.4.

16 See, eg., S.James & N.Lopez, 'A woman's place is in the Labour manifesto', *Morning Star*, 5.6.17, https://www.morningstaronline.co.uk/a-7d9a-a-womans-place-is-in-the-labour-manifesto-1.

17 Nancy Fraser, 'How feminism became capitalism's handmaiden - and how to reclaim it', *Guardian*, 14.10.13, https://www.theguardian.com/commentisfree/2013/oct/14/feminism-capitalist-handmaiden-neoliberal.

18 'Jeremy Corbyn's 10 Point Manifesto 'To Rebuild And Transform Britain', Huffington Post, 4.8.16, http://www.huffingtonpost.co.uk/entry/jeremy-corbyns-full-10-point-plan-to-rebuild-and-transform-britain_uk_57a30d8ce4b06c6e8dc6af2a.

19 Labour Party manifesto, 2017, https://labour.org.uk/manifesto/.

20 A.Dworkin, *Right wing women*, Perigee Trade, 1983.

21 English summary of the Evaluation of the ban on purchase of sexual services (1999-2008), Swedish Ministry of Justice, 2010. See also: M.Waltman, 'Prohibiting Sex Purchasing and Ending Trafficking: The Swedish Prostitution Law', *Michigan Journal of International Law*, 2011.

22 *Demand Change: Understanding the Nordic Approach to Prostitution*, Coalition Against Trafficking in Women Australia, 2013.

23 M.Waltman, 'Sweden's prohibition of purchase of sex: The law's reasons, impact, and potential', *Women's Studies International Forum*, 2011.

24 *Evaluation of the ban on purchase of sexual services*, Ministry of Justice, Government Offices of Sweden, 2.7.10, p.37.

25 'Women on corporate boards globally', Catalyst, 16.3.17, http://www.catalyst.org/knowledge/women-corporate-boards-globally.

26 'Judicial Diversity Statistics 2017', 20.7.17, https://www.judiciary.gov.uk/about-the-judiciary/who-are-the-judiciary/diversity/judicial-diversity-statistics-2017/.

27 K. Malleson, 'The case for gender quotas for appointments to the Supreme Court', UKSC blog, 23.5.14, http://ukscblog.com/case-gender-quotas-appointments-supreme-court/.

28 'Of Women: In the 21st Century by Shami Chakrabarti review', *Guardian,* 22.10.17, https://www.theguardian.com/books/2017/oct/22/of-women-in-the-21st-century-shami-chakrabarti-review-gender-inequality.

29 *An Overview of Sexual Offending in England and Wales,* the first ever joint official statistics bulletin on sexual violence released by the Ministry of Justice (MoJ), Office for National Statistics (ONS) and Home Office in January 2013.

30 L.Kelly, J.Lovett and L.Regan, *A gap or a chasm? Attrition in reported rape cases,* 2005.

31 'Reported rapes in England and Wales double in four year', *Guardian,* 13.10.16, https://www.theguardian.com/society/2016/oct/13/reported-rapes-in-england-and-wales-double-in-five-years.

32 Section 74 of the Sexual Offences Act 2003.

33 C.MacKinnon, 'Rape redefined', *Harvard Law and Policy Review,* 2016.

34 In the decision of *Akayesu* of the International Criminal Tribunal for Rwanda [Prosecutor v. Akayesu, Case No. ICTR-96-4-T, Judgment 598 (2 September 1998)] rape was redefined internationally for the first time: "a physical invasion of a sexual nature, committed on a person under circumstances which are coercive". Non/consent is absent and coercion can include a range of circumstances.

35 'Shadow education secretary Angela Rayner unveils universal childcare plans for two to four-year-olds', *Evening Standard,* 26.9.17, https://www.standard.co.uk/news/politics/shadow-education-secretary-angela-rayner-unveils-universal-childcare-plans-for-two-to-fouryearolds-a3644181.html.

36 'These 10 countries have the best parental leave policies in the world', World Economic Forum, 24.8.16, https://www.weforum.org/agenda/2016/08/these-10-countries-have-the-best-parental-leave-policies-in-the-world.

37 'Welcome to Jeremy Corbyn's blokey Britain - where 'brocialism' rules', *Telegraph,* 14.9.15, http://www.telegraph.co.uk/women/life/welcome-to-jeremy-corbyns-blokey-britain-where-brocialism-rules/.

38 'Labour's sexist above of its own is shocking, says Yvette Cooper', *Telegraph,* 26.9.15,

http://www.telegraph.co.uk/news/politics/Jeremy_Corbyn/11893926/Labours-sexist-abuse-of-its-own-is-shocking-says-Yvette-Cooper.html.

39 'Labour appoints independent expert to examine sexual harassment complaints', *Independent*, 3.11.17, http://www.independent.co.uk/news/uk/politics/labour-sexual-harassment-investigation-independent-examiners-bex-bailey-a8036501.html.

ECONOMICS, DEMOCRATISATION AND LOCALISM

The Lost World of Peter Lee

John Tomaney

There is a growing recognition that decentralisation and localism should play a key role in a future Labour manifesto. Where should Labour look for lessons about effective localism? The party's own past provides valuable lessons about how to forge a progressive localism.

County Durham emerged as a Labour heartland in the period between the First and Second World Wars, but the origins of this hegemony are poorly understood today. Labour's rise was hard-fought and by no means inevitable. Peter Lee (1864–1935) was a political colossus who, during the 1920s and 1930s, held the leading positions in both the Durham Miners' Association (DMA) and Durham County Council. He presided over Labour's rise, exercising extraordinary local political power. Today, his life and work is largely forgotten in the region he did so much to transform, albeit he is commemorated in the New Town which bears his name. But his life bears scrutiny for the light it sheds on how Labour won and used power in Durham, the strengths and limits of this politics, and its contemporary relevance.

The foundation of Labour's power was the DMA, but local politics was not simply a product of the dominance of coal. The Durham miners came relatively late to Labour. In the early twentieth century, the DMA was aligned with the Liberals. The Miners' Federation of Great Britain affiliated to Labour in 1910, the DMA not until 1919. During the 1920s and 1930s, though, Labour captured control of local government in the county and began to use it to address the neglected basic needs of working people. In his 1946 novel, *Charity Main*, a lightly fictionalised account of his time in the Durham coalfield, Mark Benney attributes Labour's ascendancy to the need to tackle the legacy of the 'coalowners' complete severance of industrial from social responsibilities'.[1] Peter Lee was the central figure in this story.

Peter Lee went down Littletown Colliery, near Durham, aged 10. In his youth, he was an itinerant drinker and fighter. He was saved by a love of books, a belated commitment to self-improvement and, above all, marriage to his childhood sweetheart, Alice Thompson. Under her influence, he gave up drink and became a Methodist preacher. The couple settled in Wheatley Hill where he took the role of checkweighman at the colliery, the trusted representative of the workforce in the determination of piece earnings.

Peter Lee began his long march through the institutions of local government in 1903, when he was elected to Wheatley Hill Parish Council. In 1907, he was elected to Easington Rural District Council, developing 'a consuming interest in the provision of water and improving sanitation'.[2] He argued for these improvements in the face of ratepayer opposition, which called his plans reckless and un-costed. His enemy was the dangerous level of diphtheria in Wheatley Hill, which were attributed to poor sanitation. He was prodigiously hard working and noted for his attention to detail. In 1909, he was elected to Durham County Council. When Labour won control of the County Council in 1919, Peter Lee was offered the role of Chairman. After returning to Wheatley Hill to discuss the offer with Alice and the DMA Lodge, he agreed to accept it: he was 55 years old. After briefly losing control of the council in 1922, Labour regained it in 1925 and has held it since. Now, according to his biographer Jack Lawson, Peter Lee assumed the role of 'chief of the civic life of Durham and leader of its people.[3] A household name locally, he could fill any hall. He was physically imposing, over six feet tall; but quiet, lacking in personal ambition and 'almost medieval in his monk-like passion for withdrawing from the world'.[4]

Peter Lee personified Morgan Phillips' proposition that the Labour Party owed more to Methodism than Marx. Politics was his sacred duty. He believed in the moral superiority of Labour, confronted with the corruption and inequity of capitalism. But he sought accommodation with capitalism rather than its overthrow. In his role as a union leader he always wanted to settle rather than prolong strikes. He was driven by an intense sense of social injustice rather than an ideology. He practised a demotic socialism focused on practical solutions to everyday problems. One of his greatest legacies arose from his obsession with the provision of clean and reliable water supplies and improved sanitation. A crisis occurred in 1914 when privately-controlled water supplies to Consett were disrupted for several weeks, representing a massive failure of 'free enterprise' to meet basic human needs. Under Peter Lee's leadership, in 1919, the existing private companies were wound up and replaced by a new publicly-owned Durham County Water Board. An early task was the building of Burnhope Reservoir in Upper Weardale. Lee proselytised for the project, sought central government funding and used the rates to pay for its construction. The building of the reservoir was a massive engineering challenge, completed in 1937, two years after the death of its originator. The provision of clean water contributed to the decline of infant mortality rates – hitherto the highest in the country – at a faster rate than anywhere else during this time. The new reservoir symbolised a far-reaching transformation of social conditions in fields such as housing, health and education.

In 1934, J.B. Priestley painted a memorably grim portrait of village life in Shotton, near to Peter Lee's Wheatley Hill.[5] But his account overlooked the forms of self-organisation that shaped these communities. Mark Benney noted in 1946 that, 'wherever, by chance, the eye rests upon some building more attractive than its neighbours, one almost invariably finds that it owes its existence to the organised efforts of the miners themselves. Their clubs, welfare institutes, and co-op stores are outstanding institutional buildings'.[6] Each village, according to the novelist Sid Chaplin, was 'a sort of self-constructed, do-it-yourself counter-environment', which the people had built themselves. Chaplin acknowledged their imperfections, such as the gendered nature of the opportunities they offered, and admitted that his greatest ambition as a youth had been to escape. But he insisted, 'their achievements cry out for celebration'.[7] Peter Lee and other Labour leaders drew on these traditions, but added to them the power of the nascent local state.

Peter Lee was deeply localist: 'Many times he was invited to stand for Parliament. But instinctively he knew his own unique value in the North, so he stayed there'.[8] An inveterate walker and cyclist, he had a deep knowledge of the northern landscape and culture: 'Local history and legend were probed for his purpose. An ancient lead mine, a farm, or church built of stones from old Roman ramparts told a story'.[9] He loved Durham Cathedral deeply and its associations with St Cuthbert and St Bede, despite his Methodist faith. He belonged profoundly to Durham. The miners' Lodge remained the key political institution, but a politics of community and belonging was being forged alongside workplace struggles, best expressed in the annual Miners' Gala, 'the spontaneous expression of communal life'.[10]

Of course, we cannot recreate the world of Peter Lee, but County Durham remains a Labour heartland, in part, because it still draws on the diminishing moral and physical capital accumulated during the era of Peter Lee, when local state power was used relentlessly to address the basic needs of local communities in the face of neglect and opposition from the privileged. Today, the region abounds in unmet human needs. There is a yearning for community and belonging, and a space for a politics that recognises this. The extraordinary contemporary revival of the Miners' Gala, with its modern pageant of bands and banners, is one powerful testament to this. The lost world of Peter Lee was more divided internally, along religious, cultural and material lines, and more susceptible to media narratives than we realise today. Workplace solidarity and community cohesion were not bequeathed to Labour but were hard won. Labour's local task was achieving compromise about policy priorities focused on the foundational requirements of civilised life, in the process balancing different interests and identities. Labour's own history provides plenty of food for thought to inform a modern, progressive localism.

John Tomaney is Professor of Urban and Regional Planning in the Bartlett School of Planning, University College London.

This article is based on a commission by the Durham Book Festival 2017. Thanks to Florence Sutcliffe-Braithwaite, Ross Forbes, Jonathan Renouf and Kate Tomaney for comments on an earlier draft.

Notes

1 M. Benney, *Charity Main: A Coalfield Chronicle*, George Allen and Unwin, 1946.

2 W. A. Moyes, *Mostly Mining: A Study of the Development of Easington Rural District from the Earliest Times*, Frank Graham, 1969.

3 J. Lawson, *Peter Lee*, The Epworth Press, 1946, p130.

4 Lawson, *Peter Lee*, p105.

5 J. B. Priestley, *An English Journey*, William Heinemann/Victor Gollancz, 1934.

6 Benney, *Charity Main*, p51.

7 S. Chaplin, 'Durham mining villages', in M. Bulmer, ed., *Mining and Social Change. Durham County in the Twentieth Century*, Croom Helm, 1978, pp81, 71.

8 Lawson, *Peter Lee*, p157.

9 Lawson, *Peter Lee*, p111.

10 Lawson, *Peter Lee*, p168.

Peter Lee and Localism Today

Rachel Reeves

Peter Lee offers an example of Labour politics rooted in a local community and founded on finding practical solutions to local problems. To follow his example today, Labour needs to work to localise power, build an industrial strategy based on the needs of the everyday economy and democratise the way our economy works.

In recounting Peter Lee's story, John Tomaney offers a powerful account of the source and character of Labour's strength in one of its traditional heartlands. Many of these communities, especially in the North East and Midlands, detached from global growth and benefiting least from the knowledge and creative economies, have been drifting away from Labour since midway through the last decade, a process which continued – despite our success in Britain's cities and university towns – in June 2017.[1] All too often, in Tomaney's evocative phrase, the party hangs on thanks to the 'diminishing moral and physical capital accumulated' by past generations.

My own predecessor as Leeds MP, Alice Bacon, grew up in in the febrile atmosphere of a West Yorkshire mining town in the run-up to the General Strike of 1926. Raised by a father immersed in trade union activism, local politics and community leadership, Alice recalled that 'there was never a time when I decided to join the Labour Party' – she was born into it.[2] For someone like her, to join Labour was 'as natural as breathing'.[3] It is hard to imagine that would be true of many working-class girls growing up in a town like Normanton today.

Historically, Labour's strength in towns and villages across County Durham, Yorkshire and elsewhere was rooted in a claim to represent the working people of those communities. That didn't just mean representation in terms of their material and social needs, but also in a proximity and sensitivity to local culture and identity. Communities aren't static, and Labour needs to be in step with social change; we are a more diverse society, and the importance of taking into account gender, sexuality and ethnic diversity when we think about identity and equality is – thankfully – far more widely acknowledged than it was in the first half of the twentieth century. In part, recovering Labour's closeness to the communities it seeks to represent is about ensuring that the party, at every level, from councillors and activists to the Shadow Cabinet, is more representative of them. It means working closely alongside local groups trying to improve those communities – whether it is local trade union branches, faith groups, or campaigns like that in my own constituency in Leeds West, to preserve local institutions like the Bramley Baths and Library – as well as articulating Labour's priorities in a way that speaks to the way people feel about work, family and place.

As Tomaney and Ruth Davis have argued, these values can sit comfortably alongside – and provide a basis for – an inclusive, egalitarian, green politics.[4] Work, especially, needs to be considered not as a source of drudgery to be replaced in an automated, post-work future, but – when properly regulated and remunerated – as a source of meaning, autonomy and dignity.[5] Labour, after all, was created as the party of work, to give a voice to ordinary, working-class people in Parliament.

To deliver good work and prosperous, interconnected communities, an appreciation of everyday values and experiences must be married to a radical political economy. As Tomaney tells us, Peter Lee 'practiced a demotic socialism focused on practical solutions to every day problems', such as the provision of clean water and decent housing. Labour's early pioneers in local and municipal government placed front-and-centre issues like these, which formed the basis of the everyday economy: those sectors which provide the foundation for our everyday lives. Alongside the provision of utilities and housing, this includes health and social care, education and retail parts of our economy.

We need to better consider what today's equivalents are of those causes which animated our forebears in the late nineteenth- and early twentieth century.

Some – such as housing and the need for security in work – are not new at all. Others have emerged or grown in salience more recently, like the need for far more expansive systems of care provision, or for the overhaul of the most bureaucratic and disempowering parts of our welfare state, like the Work Capability Assessment. And like Labour's early leaders, we need a vision of politics that goes beyond material concerns. Our epidemics of loneliness and mental illness relate to the increasingly disconnected nature of our society, and progressive politics should offer an answer to this.[6]

The everyday economy, and especially care, will provide a huge – and increasing – number of jobs in the future, disproportionately filled by women. However, these sectors also frequently suffer from low productivity, and offer low wages and insecure working conditions. The benefits to the people working in these sectors from an industrial policy concentrated on advanced manufacturing are limited. An industrial strategy with the everyday economy at its heart can drive up living standards and bring politics closer to those communities excluded from the benefits of the thriving, globalised parts of the modern economy.

That requires an agenda based around regional banks to spread capital to all our regions, and the devolution of further power and resources. It also means thinking about how we can encourage advances in management and the uptake of technology in sectors like retail and care, in ways which improve rather than displace jobs. The Fabian Society's Retail Taskforce offered a wealth of ideas for improving wages, conditions, productivity and workers' autonomy in the sector, from the creation of a 'super skills council' and a new Catapult Centre for management, to a crackdown on monopolistic activities by major retailers and measures to increase worker voice.[7] Britain needs an enabling state which supports alternative models of ownership and the provision of public services and utilities, such as renewable energy cooperatives, credit unions and schemes to support lonely or ill people. We need to empower local authorities to do more, and unleash their potential to build wealthier, more equal, more resilient, happier communities.

Where possible, power over the everyday economy should be devolved to our regions, towns and cities, bringing them closer to the people. However, it cannot just be devolution to local authorities. Councils in turn must devolve power within their communities, use their powers of procurement to foster vibrant models of co-operative, mutual or community ownership to empower workers and consumers, and work with anchor institutions, whether it is the local hospital, a major private sector employer, or a global university. Labour needs to understand the capacity of the state not just to regulate and redistribute from above, but to bring together and support stakeholders in their local communities to work for the common good.[8]

On a local level, working within the narrow confines of the powers and resources which local authorities are allowed, we can see examples of this kind of politics, such as Preston's strategy for community wealth-building, Leeds' neighbourhood networks to help older people live independent, fulfilling lives, and Hammersmith and Fulham's new industrial strategy.[9] Think tanks like the Centre for Local Economic Strategies and the new Centre for Towns, and initiatives like the RSA's recent Inclusive Growth Commission and IPPR's Commission on Economic Justice, have begun to outline a new approach to the economy, based around place, regional equality and more democratic forms of ownership and decision-making.

Lee's story reminds us of the need for a politics connected to the everyday lives of the people Labour seeks to represent. That rests on three pillars. First – as we saw in June 2017 – a guarantee that Government will invest in the public services, small businesses and homes that our communities rely on. Second, a language that speaks to people's everyday lives and the things that matter to them: family, place and work. Finally, we need to offer a new approach to the central and local state, which seeks to empower communities and help them build the institutions and capacities needed for resilience and prosperity going forward.

Peter Lee was rooted in his community and dedicated to improving the everyday lives of the men and women within it. To broaden Labour's coalition to win, but more importantly to ensure that we are relevant in our heartland communities, we could do a lot worse than looking to his example.

Rachel Reeves is MP for Leeds West, Chair of the Business, Energy and Industrial Strategy Select Committee and Co-Chair of the Jo Cox Commission on Loneliness. She is the author of *Alice in Westminster: The Political Life of Alice Bacon*.

Notes

1 W. Jennings and G. Stoker, 'Tilting Towards the Cosmopolitan Axis?: Political Change in England and the 2017 General Election', *Political Quarterly*, 88, 2017..
2 R. Reeves, *Alice in Westminster: The Political Life of Alice Bacon*, IB Tauris, 2016, p21.
3 Ibid, p28.
4 J. Tomaney, 'Parochialism: A Defence', *Progress in Human Geography*, 37, 2013; R. Davis, 'Home is Where the Heart is', *Fabian Review*, 128, 2016.
5 R. Yeoman, 'Conceptualising Work as a Fundamental Human Need', *Journal of Business Ethics*, 125, 2014.
6 R. Reeves, 'Throwing a New Light on Loneliness', speech to Policy Exchange, 11.12.17.
7 C. Tait, *At the Crossroads: The Future of UK Retail*, Fabian Society, 2016.
8 See, for instance, J. Wilson, *Letting Go*, Fabian Society, 2012.
9 *Community Wealth-Building through Anchor Institutions*, Centre for Local Economic Strategies, 2017; *Economic Growth for Everyone: An Industrial Strategy for Hammersmith and Fulham*, Hammersmith and Fulham Borough Council, 2017.

Alternatives to State-Socialism in Britain: Other Worlds of Labour in the Twentieth Century

Alastair Reid

Our new volume *Alternatives to State Socialism in Britain* (edited along with Peter Ackers) charts associations, leaders and intellectuals who have sought to encourage participatory and decentralised forms of politics, rooted in local communities. This history provides a vital tradition for Labour to draw on, showing how localist perspectives might invigorate the party's emerging critique of contemporary capitalism.

In recent years, many on the left of Labour have called for the party to roll back what they see as New Labour's accommodation with the legacy of Thatcherism. In policy terms – not least in the party's highly successful 2017 manifesto – this has generally centred on reasserting the primacy of the state, to counter the sharper edges of an increasingly marketised society. However, the Corbyn-led Labour Party *also* aspires to be a social movement, emphasising decentralization, localism, grassroots campaigning and civil society.

'Blue Labour' thinkers, meanwhile, continue to advance an alternative viewpoint, arguing that the statism of not only Corbynism but *also* Blairism is representative of longer deficiencies in left thought. For example, in Maurice

Glasman's account, the post-1945 settlement's emphasis on collective bargaining between the state and trade unions eroded older mutualist traditions of self-help.[1] Civil society, it is held, holds the key to re-engaging with communities forgotten by the rarefied, technocratic modern left.

Both of these accounts have their merits. The period from 1918 to 1979 was indeed broadly dominated by the new mass politics of industrial society, as working people successfully staked a claim for the state to protect the working classes from the vagaries of the market. This 'state socialism' set the agenda for much of the twentieth century, until Margaret Thatcher turned the tide towards the market in the period since the late-1970s. But our new volume *Alternatives to State Socialism in Britain* (edited along with Peter Ackers) analyses another important tradition of organising, from the late-nineteenth century right through to the present day.[2] It charts associations, leaders and intellectuals who have sought to encourage participatory and decentralised forms of politics, rooted in local communities. This alternative history provides a vital tradition for Labour to draw on, and in particular shows how localist perspectives might invigorate the party's emerging critique of contemporary capitalism.

Voluntary traditions, voluntary associations

Voluntarism and localism were crucial tenets of organised labour in the early to mid-twentieth century. Trade unions not only bargained with the state, but also worked collaboratively, amongst themselves *and* with employers – securing important advances in working conditions as a result. Leaders such as Walter Citrine, general secretary of the Trade Union Congress from 1926 to 1946, actively steered their unions away from the politics of direct action, and towards a more constructive engagement with local government and partnerships with progressive employers; people such as Edward Cadbury, the enlightened Quaker owner of the famous chocolate producer.[3] Citrine's emphasis on decentralised work by unions to deliver improvements in workers' pay and conditions, meant establishing a gap between the unions and the Labour Party, because the unions represented members of all political parties. It also meant a willingness to have meaningful negotiations with employers, most notably in the case of the extensive 'Mond-Turner' talks in the aftermath of the 1926 'General Strike'.[4]

Co-operatives and local voluntary associations also remained central to the pursuit of progressive aims. It is worth remembering that in 1945 the membership of British retail cooperative societies was around the same size as that of the country's trade unions, both involving between 9 and 10 million people. After 1945 the Co-operative Party resisted any proposal that its affiliated organisations could be used to administer forms of national public monopoly, and it continued to insist instead that any participation in cooperation should be based on the voluntary principle.[5] And the beliefs of the co-operative movement were part of an emerging critique of the post-war settlement's statism.[6] If the Institute for Workers' Control, founded in 1968, provided a forceful, utopian-socialist attack on the bureaucracy of corporatist Britain,[7] then their efforts were preceded by liberal industrial-relations theorists such as Hugh Clegg and Alan Flanders. In particular Clegg's policy work stressed that strikes were caused by inflexible management – more faith should be given to trade union members to elaborate agreements on their own terms.[8]

The power of decentralisation and grassroots campaigning is also seen in the work of working-class women activists in the first half of the twentieth century, who were able to achieve improvements in the provision of social services through their participation in local voluntary organisations, district councils and borough councils. They were highly attentive to the particular form such provision took, because they knew from their own experience about the needs and attitudes of the working-class service users. They wanted more participation, not just for themselves, but for all the working women they represented: so they were also active campaigners for birth control and adult education.[9] In later decades the voluntary sector would expand to offer care for the most disadvantaged groups in society, such as the elderly and the disabled, as well as 'supplementing' state provision through hospice care, playgroups, and initiatives like the Citizens' Advice Bureau.[10]

Even at the high point of state-socialism then, civil society – particularly at a local level – provided an important site where activists worked for important progressive outcomes. For many, from the 1970s the Thatcherite attack on institutions of the state was felt profoundly shockingly. But those who stood within the tradition sketched out here also shared Thatcher's longer-term concern about the impersonal and bureaucratic nature of centralised social policies. The wave of 1960s community activism highlighted what many ordinary people already knew – that state provision of welfare and housing was substandard, and that users of public services were often marginalized and disempowered.[11]

This dissatisfaction spun off into a range of important localist solutions.[12] The pragmatic anarchist Colin Ward had long been championing grass-roots collective self-help in housing provision: supporting squatting in empty properties, housing cooperatives, and self-build, even up to the level of 'Do-It-Yourself New Towns'. Meanwhile, consciously echoing the revival of movements for workers' control in the sphere of employment, the socialist-feminist Sheila Rowbotham called for community control of children's nurseries, within which parents would obviously be well placed to make a creative contribution. From 1981, these strands coalesced around the Labour-controlled Greater London Council (GLC), as it supported a range of creative local initiatives which bolstered a sense not only of community, but of diversity and tolerance. Instead of aiming for a greatly reduced public sector, thinkers such as these were broadly agreed in proposing that central government should continue to raise revenues and redistribute resources. However, the use to which these resources were put should be decided through democratic participation at the local level; and the inevitably resulting diversity of provision should be welcomed.

Alternatives to state socialism today

The tradition (or traditions) of voluntarism, localism, civil society and community activism that we analyse in *Alternatives to State-Socialism* remains important. After years of confusion and disorientation, the left appears to be making steps towards reenergising the cause of eradicating inequality, and empowering ordinary people. But we want to warn against the idea that this involves returning to a supposedly 'real British Socialism' before New Labour. The principal source of such nostalgia is the 1945 Labour government. This faced massive post-war reconstruction problems and, in those trying economic and social circumstances, introduced important reforms that, by and large, improved the lives of ordinary working people. It used policies—such as nationalisation—that were in vogue then to address the problems of that time, and deserves all credit for its long-term achievements, such as full employment and a more generous welfare safety net.

But there were losses as well as gains. The involvement of women and immigrants, for example, in local voluntary associations, or participatory schemes run by the GLC, in contrast to the initiatives of the central state, illustrates the narrowness of much traditional social democracy. Similar questions hang over other large-scale, centralised one-stop 'solutions' to inequality, such as comprehensive education and the NHS.[13] On closer inspection, the state-socialist blueprints for a better society have not been the comprehensive success that some claim, and the current predilection for gigantic, impersonal schools and hospitals suggests that few lessons have been learned from the constructive post-war critics.

Even so, many on the left today would argue that the only alternative to state-socialism is capitulation to neo-liberalism and the spread of private profit and market solutions. Setting aside for a moment the genuine benefits markets may bring wherever we need to know what goods and services people really want, this argument ignores the third sector of civil society: the community organizations and associational life that figure in our collection.

Cooperatives, mutuals and other associational forms could still play a much larger role in our current society: delivering business goods and services, health, education and housing, as well as providing opportunities for participatory citizenship. We can revive consumers' and producers' cooperatives, using co-operation to influence markets in progressive directions. One key way Labour could use the state at the local level to encourage co-operatives is by leveraging the massive purchasing power of anchor institutions like local government, hospitals and FE colleges to drive the sort of economic models we want to see.[14]

We can try to build partnerships between employers and employees within the workplace – throughout modern British history, as the case of Edward Cadbury shows, this has proven a highly successful way of ensuring working conditions and decent pay, and enshrining best practice. Trade unions must be prepared to adapt to their members' needs – and on this, they have shown that they are willing to do so, through new models of organizing and consultation including the highly effective provision of individual legal services and an increasing engagement with social media.

Public ownership is back on the agenda, driven by Jeremy Corbyn and organizations such as We Own It. But we can learn from earlier critiques of unresponsive state bureaucracies and think about new models of public ownership and social ownership that are more responsive to citizens' needs and desires.[15] And finally, we should seek to build on user participation in the shaping of local social services, just as, for example, the GLC was able to deliver in its innovative community initiatives. All of these options provide ways to temper the worst excesses of the market whilst avoiding the brittleness of statism, and also giving ordinary people a real stake in the organization of society.

The value of localism

Blue Labour thinkers have also mooted that re-engaging with civil society, or the 'local', might serve as a way to reconnect with 'traditional' working-class cultures otherwise 'left behind' by contemporary politics.[16] But what we *also* hope to have shown is that radical localism is not about tapping into rather fixed, traditional cultural worlds in order to mobilise them in support of a new national project.[17] Rather it is based on an explicit political critique of power relations, broadly inherited from the nineteenth-century liberal tradition. In this respect it is a serious defect in Blue Labour thinking to equate liberalism with the free market, resulting in a misunderstanding of so-called 'neo-liberalism' and the forfeiting of opportunities to connect with other, non-Labour, currents of public opinion.[18]

Indeed, a traditional liberal perspective dramatically highlights the highly centralised nature of the UK system of parliamentary representation, which offers real opportunities to both right-wing authoritarians and left-wing reformers to seize power at the centre and direct national affairs in a decisive way. This has, on the whole, been the style of the sequence of Prime Ministers since Margaret Thatcher who have all, moreover, contributed to the further centralisation of the way in which the state apparatus in Westminster and Whitehall itself is run. Our collection points to an equally important and deeply-rooted current of decentralisation which has become relatively overlooked and forgotten, one based around a vibrant tradition of voluntary associations, both local and national. As these issues seemingly once more receive attention, we hope that re-engaging with this strand of popular self-organisation will help all progressive forces to clarify their strategies, and to once more empower ordinary people, wherever they live.

Alastair J Reid is a historian and Life Fellow of Girton College, Cambridge. He is co-editor, with Peter Ackers, of *Alternatives to State Socialism in Britain (2017)*.

Notes

1 M. Glasman, 'Labour as a radical tradition', *Soundings*, 46, 2010.

2 P. Ackers and A. Reid eds., *Alternatives to State Socialism in Britain: Other Worlds of Labour in the Twentieth Century*, Palgrave MacMillan, 2017.

3 J. Kimberley, 'Edward Cadbury: An Egalitarian Employer and Supporter of Working Women's Campaigns', in *Alternatives to State Socialism.*

4 J. Moher, 'Walter Citrine: A Union Pioneer of Industrial Cooperation', in *Alternatives to State Socialism.*

5 R. Vorberg-Rugh and Angela Whitecross, 'The Co-operative Party: An Alternative Vision of Social Ownership', in *Alternatives to State Socialism.*

6 R. Whiting, 'Trade Unions: Voluntary Associations and Individual Rights', in *Alternatives to State Socialism.*

7 J. Guinan, 'Bring Back the Institute for Workers' Control', *Renewal*, 23:4, 2015.

8 P. Ackers, 'Collective bargaining as industrial democracy: Hugh Clegg and the political foundations of British industrial relations pluralism', *British Journal of Industrial Relations*, 45, 2007.

9 R. Davidson, 'Working-Class Women Activists: Citizenship at the Local Level', in *Alternatives to State Socialism.*

10 P. Alcock, 'Voluntary action, New Labour and the "third sector"', in M. Hilton and J. McKay, eds, *The Ages of Voluntarism: How we got to the Big Society*, Oxford University Press, 2011; P. Thane, 'Voluntary action in Britain since Beveridge', in M. Oppenheimer and N. Deakin, eds, *Beveridge and Voluntary Action in Britain and the Wider British World*, Manchester: Manchester University Press, 2011.

11 D. Ellis, 'On taking (back) control: lessons from Community Action in 1970s Britain', *Renewal*, 25:1, 2017.

12 S. White, 'The Left After Social Democracy: Towards State–Society Partnerships', in *Alternatives to State Socialism.*

13 S. Hutchinson, 'Protecting the legacy: developing a Labour vision for health and

social care', *Renewal*, 25:3-4, 2017; S. Iliffe and R. Bourne, 'The NHS: not back to Era 1 but forward to Era 3 – policy challenges for Labour', *Renewal*, 25:1, 2016.

14 Matthew Brown and Martin O'Neill, 'The Road to Socialism is the A59: The Preston Model', *Renewal*, 24:2, 2016.

15 Labour Party, *Alternative models of ownership*, 2017.

16 For example: D. Goodhart, *The Road to Somewhere: The Populist Revolt and the Future of Politics*, C Hurst & Co., 2017.

17 On the deficiencies of purely cultural analyses of class, see: E. Gibbs, 'Who's "Normal"? Class, Culture and Labour Politics in a Fragmented Britain', *Renewal*, 25:1, 2017.

18 For a concise account of the varieties of liberal thought, see M. Freeden, *Liberalism. A Very Short Introduction*, Oxford:Oxford University Press, 2015.